Gestalt The...

Gestalt Therapy
Theory, practice and research

Eleanor O'Leary

Lecturer, University College, Cork, Ireland

with the collaboration of
Wanda Knopek

CHAPMAN & HALL

London · Glasgow · New York · Tokyo · Melbourne · Madras

Published by Chapman & Hall, 2–6 Boundary Row, London SE1 8HN

Chapman & Hall, 2–6 Boundary Row, London SE1 8HN, UK

Blackie Academic & Professional, Wester Cleddens Road, Bishopbriggs, Glasgow G64 2NZ, UK

Chapman & Hall, 29 West 35th Street, New York NY10001, USA

Chapman & Hall Japan, Thomson Publishing Japan, Hirakawacho Nemoto Building, 6F, 1–7–11 Hirakawa-cho, Chiyoda-ku, Tokyo 102, Japan

Chapman & Hall Australia, Thomas Nelson Australia, 102 Dodds Street, South Melbourne, Victoria 3205, Australia

Chapman & Hall India, R. Seshadri, 32 Second Main Road, CIT East, Madras 600 035, India

Distributed in the USA and Canada by Singular Publishing Group Inc., 4284 41st Street, San Diego, California 92105

First edition 1992

© 1992 Chapman & Hall

Typeset in 10 on 12pt Palatino by Acorn Bookwork, Salisbury, England
Printed in Great Britain at T.J. Press, (Padstow) Ltd, Padstow, Cornwall

ISBN 0 412 43510 1   1 56593 036 3 (USA)

Contents

TO MY PARENTS, JACK AND JOAN O'LEARY

Acknowledgements

First and foremost to Fr Brian Kelly, my friend, who has been the most influential person in my academic life.

I wish to pay special tribute to two fine scholars, Professors Carl Thoresen, Stanford University, and Ron Fredrickson, University of Massachusetts, Amherst, for whose generous help I am very grateful.

I am also happy to acknowledge the following: Noreen Sweeny, John McCarthy, Michael Crowley, Dr Art Berger and my uncle Martin Murphy for their critical comments; Dr Alice Elliott and Celia Mooers Squires of Media-Psych, San Diego for allowing me to reproduce the script of the Impasse film by Fritz Perls; Drs Travis Tatum and Alan Eccleston, Bernadette Morgan and Jerry Lynch for their co-operation; Rosemary Morris and the staff at Chapman & Hall, for their unstinting help in the final preparation of this book; Rita McCarthy and Mary O'Sullivan who so willingly typed the various drafts; some very special people in my life; my sister Joan, brothers John and Bob, their families, and many others whose support and friendship is a welcome counterbalance to the gravity of my academic pursuits.

Finally, my greatest thanks must go to Wanda Knopek, my collaborator, who was thorough in the work she undertook, and whose skill as a gestalt therapist and grasp of theoretical issues made her the ideal person for the task.

Foreword

In the philosophy of science two contexts of inquiry are often considered: contexts of discovery and confirmation. In the discovery context the processes are mostly creative and divergent, such as constructing conjectures, altering concepts and revising theory. Research studies during this phase are typically small scale, often descriptive case studies – some of them experimental in design – or correlational.

The processes gradually shift to a more confirmatory approach, with larger scale studies that try to control for alternative interpretations that could explain the data. Confirmatory processes seek to demonstrate that stated hypotheses and their supporting conceptual frameworks are valid and believable (some might say are 'proved true').

Scientists however, as human beings, seldom, if ever, behave in a linear straightforward fashion. Instead, they jump around, going back and forth between continuing to discover and trying to confirm. This oscillation takes place in part because of what Pascal, the 17th century mathematician, observed: 'the more we come to know, the more we come to realize what we do not know'.

In many ways, the art and the science of gestalt approaches to therapy are still very much in the context of discovery. Basic concepts and assumptions of gestalt therapy, such as contacting inner experiences, sensory oriented awareness, types of boundaries, and unfinished business, while clinically rich, remain very loose and open-ended, subject to a variety of interpretations. Many conjectures, some possibly contradictory of others, await confirmation. Must all persons, for example, contact their inner experience through sensory processes to change in meaningful ways? Techniques commonly used, such as dream work, the empty chair, and the small group format – procedures not unique to gestalt therapy – also await confirmation from controlled experiments demonstrating their effectiveness. Gestalt therapy from a scientific perspective, broadly construed, remains highly promising but not confirmed.

Many of the premises and procedures of gestalt therapy strike me as very dynamic, rich with possibilities. A weekend 'seminar' with Fritz Perls at Esalen in the late 1960s introduced me to this dynamic if not demanding approach. Despite my enthusiasm I have some doubts – call it a healthy skepticism – that much of what is currently believed about gestalt therapy will hold up when well-controlled experimental studies are conducted. As with almost all approaches to counselling and therapy, the processes of scientific inquiry will yield, over time, changes in how gestalt therapy is conceptualized and conducted.

Eleanor O'Leary has written I believe an excellent introduction to gestalt therapy. She clearly recognizes the need for excellence not only in the clinical practice of gestalt therapy but in improvement of theory as well as research. In noting that 'gestalt therapy is still in its infancy', she recognizes that its infancy has been prolonged by the lack of good science, that is the scarcity of carefully conceived empirical studies that challenge the major assumptions in gestalt therapy. Just as a good gestalt therapist skillfully seeks to frustrate the client, to confront and challenge, researchers need to probe and push the validity of assumptions and techniques used in gestalt therapy. Clearly it is *not* a question of doing more studies *per se* but instead studies that will improve clinical practice and clarify theoretical assumptions.

She offers several suggestions for such improvement. Significantly, O'Leary brings to this book extensive clinical and training experiences in gestalt therapy. She has a solid and thorough grasp of the background and development of gestalt approaches as well as major areas and topics deserving careful study. Besides describing the beginnings of gestalt therapy, essentially the work of Fritz Perls, she provides some excellent descriptions from case material of how several techniques are used. In addition, she offers constructive suggestions for improving the quality of research, such as the need for using more than only self-report questionnaires to assess improvement coupled with longer term follow-up studies. In all, she offers a comprehensive introduction touching on several major topics.

I believe one of the most significant qualities of gestalt therapy, distinguishing it from other perspectives, lies in the recognition of how behaviour, affect and emotions, and thoughts are experienced together in specific situations. O'Leary recognizes this quality as a major strength of gestalt therapy. This focus on 'person–environment interactions' rather than just selected behaviour or thoughts is too often ignored or minimized in most therapies, fostering a prolonged verbal 'aboutism' and intellectualizing that can go on for years. Genuine and lasting change in persons demands that we deal with the give and take of behaviour, feelings, thoughts and changing contexts.

Implied in O'Leary's discussion is an emerging recognition that each person functions as an ongoing and intimate part of their environment, in what I would call an 'I–We' relationship. For too long the culturally sanctioned myth of each person as a fully autonomous, independent, 'rugged' individualist has gone unchallenged. The negative, if not tragic, consequences of this self-absorbed, quasi-narcissistic vision of the person has been demonstrated in a variety of social and physical health problems. We are all profoundly *inter*dependent, part and parcel of each other's experiences and lives. Much of gestalt therapy, as described by O'Leary, seems well positioned to help clients gain the kind of interdependent perspectives they need to fashion an optimally healthy lifestyle.

I hope readers of this book will consider seriously adapting the scientist–practitioner approach recommended by O'Leary in their work in gestalt therapy. Doing so may foster an evolution in gestalt therapy toward the 'figure' being an I–We and Thou relationship.

Carl E. Thoresen
Professor of Psychology
Stanford University

Introduction

Much has been written on gestalt therapy, yet there is an obvious need for an overview which contains the theory, research and practice of gestalt therapy. To help achieve this, its origins and their influence on its subsequent development are briefly considered. Gestalt-related concepts, goals and processes are elucidated. Particular attention is devoted to the role of experiment, dreams and fantasies, and other techniques such as the use of language and non-verbal communication. Research to date is reviewed and emerging issues are explored. Consequently the discussion has significant academic value, while still giving practical guidelines to the aspiring therapist.

The contribution of Fritz Perls is ageless. His ideas still cause debate, stimulate research and are applied internationally in the therapeutic setting. Gestalt therapy is valuable because of the contribution it makes toward mental wellbeing and social development. Perls, Hefferline and Goodman (1951) stated that 'more and more of the patients are not "sick" at all, they make adequate adjustments, they have come because they want something more out of themselves and they believe that psychotherapy can help them' (p. 310).

Gestalt therapy can deal with a wide range of emotions such as grief, anger, depression, resentment, envy, jealousy, fear and guilt. It enables people to manage these emotions through directly experiencing or expressing them anew in a recreation of the unfinished situation. The inability to let go of them is often the main obstacle to growth and development.

Chapter 1

Gestalt therapy: influences and birth

INFLUENCES ON GESTALT THERAPY

A discussion of gestalt therapy without reference to Fritz Perls and his background is like a production of Hamlet without the Prince of Denmark. The contribution of Fritz Perls is ageless. His ideas still cause debate, stimulate research and are applied internationally in the therapeutic setting.

Background influences

Fritz Perls was born Frederick Salomon Perls in Berlin on July 8, 1893. The facts concerning his family life are scanty. Born to Jewish parents, the youngest of three children, his family moved from a Jewish neighbourhood into a more fashionable part of Berlin when he was 3 years old. His parents fought frequently, to the extent that his father beat his mother. The grandparents on his mother's side were orthodox, while his father, Nathan, was what Perls (1969a) referred to as an 'assimilated' Jew, who attended temple only on the high holy days. Perls declared, 'I could not go along with this hypocrisy, and rather early declared myself an atheist'. Eventually he stated in his autobiography *In and out of the garbage pail*, 'All religions were man-made crudities, all philosophies were man-made fitting games. I had to take responsibility for myself'.

His early schooling was pedestrian. He failed the seventh grade twice and was expelled from school for misbehaviour. By the age of 14, he had enrolled in another school. Here he came to love some of the teachers, who accepted his independent ways, encouraged his interest in the theatre and offered him positive feedback. In 1916 he joined the German army and served as a medical officer in World War I.

He had two sisters, Grete, 1½ years his senior, whom he dearly loved, and Else, 3 years his senior, whose death in a concentration camp he did not grieve. Shepard (1976) points out that Perls' reference to Grete in his autobiography concerns those maternal qualities of affection through sustenance. His words concerning Else are cold: 'I disliked Else, my eldest sister. She was a clinger and I always felt uncomfortable in her presence'. After World War I, he lived with his mother and Else. By the mid 1920s he had ceased communicating with his father.

Two uncles are referred to – his mother's brother, Julius, whom he described as an 'unpretentious warm person', and her other brother, Herman Staub, the pride of the family; in Perls' (1969) view he was 'Germany's greatest legal theoretician'. It was expected that Perls would follow in Staub's footsteps, but he rebelled.

Perls discovered that this illustrious uncle had raped Perls' friend Lucy when she was 13. This brought about the judgement from Perls: 'All that façade of respectability'; yet he used this uncle to rationalize his own promiscuous behaviour by stating that the secret life of Herman Staub gave him a licence, almost a demand, to follow his example. It appears that his responsibility for himself did not encompass responsibility to others. Although married to Lore (alias Laura), a gestalt psychologist, he seemed to think nothing of having affairs. Becoming aware of one's own feelings and acting true to them without apologies was the only lesson he seemed to be trying to teach.

Lore came into his life in 1926 while working as an assistant to Kurt Goldstein, a noted gestalt psychologist. Perls refers to his marriage insensitively: 'At that time Lore pressed for marriage. I knew I was not the marrying type. I was not madly in love with her, but we had many interests in common and often had a good time'. This suggestion implies an indifference and irresponsibility on his part for the decision.

Lore and Fritz had two children, Renate (1931) and Steve (1935). Shepard (1976) sums up his role as a father in these words: 'Fritz had a justly deserved reputation for being indifferent, at best, to children and was a failure as a father' (p. 97). This was not the case for the first 4 years of Renate's life. She stated, 'Fritz adored me. He carried me around on his shoulders and showed me to everybody' (Shepard, 1976, p. 45). Perls (1969a) suggested that his change of behaviour was the result of being blamed for anything that went wrong, thus causing him to withdraw from the role as paterfamilias.

Towards the end of his autobiography he speaks of his daughter in a similar vein to that of his sister Else. Renate had written to him with pictures of her daughter, Leslie; his comment was 'For once a letter without asking me for something, but I am sure the letter is an overture for a request that likely will come via Lore'. He does, however, seem to have been fond of Leslie, whom he describes as a 'cute and bright copperhead' with 'something real about her'.

Much of what was to become Perls' theory derived from Freud, Reich, Friedlander, gestalt psychology and existentialism. Each of these influences will be traced.

Psychoanalysis and gestalt therapy

Perls was educated both at the University of Freiburg and Frederick Wilhelm University in Berlin, from where he obtained his MD in 1921. He then trained in psychoanalysis at the Psychoanalytic Institutes of Berlin, Frankfurt and Vienna. He met Freud only once after he had emigrated to South Africa. Perls (1969a) described his relationship with Freud as polemic. He stated, 'My admiration, bewilderment and vindictiveness was very strong – I am deeply awed by how much, practically all alone he achieved with inadequate mental tools of association psychology and mechanistically oriented philosophy'. Gestalt therapy adopted one crucial assumption of psychoanalysis: that by being involved with a therapist, individuals may bring into consciousness or awareness feelings, experiences and behaviours. This allows them to overcome neurotic manifestations of personality.

Naranjo (1970) points out that the first step towards Perls' concern with the present was made in Freud's observation of transference. He stated 'although at first the analysis of the present was a tool or a means for the interpretation of the past, many today regard the analysis of childhood events as a means toward the understanding of present dynamics'. Perls used Freud's concept of the unconscious, but spoke of it as that of which we are unaware.

Perls Hefferline and Goodman (1951) accepted Freud's understanding of emotions, namely that they were underlying drives that had evolved over the centuries. Perls identified two basic drives: self-preservation and species preservation, which correspond to what Freud (1975) terms 'ego instinct' and 'sexual instincts'. Freud, however, combined both these instincts under the heading of *eros*.

However, what clearly distinguished psychoanalysis and gestalt therapy was their time emphasis. While Freud viewed the first 5 years as crucial to subsequent personality development, Perls (1969b) believed that what was important was the individual's current experience.

Reich and gestalt therapy

Perls trained as a medical doctor and then as a psychoanalyst with Wilhelm Reich, and had supervision under Otto Fenichal and Karen Horney. Horney and Reich gave Perls a sense of a therapeutic relationship which could operate with a minimum of the traditional clinical routines. Horney he described as 'one of the few people I really trusted'. Horney's words to Perls as related by him (1969a) are significant: 'The only analyst that I think could get through to you would be Wilhelm Reich'. Consequently he was in analysis with Reich in 1931 and 1932, and participated in a seminar which Reich gave in 1933. The picture Perls presents of Reich is a dynamic one. He was, according to Perls, 'vital, alive, rebellious' and 'eager to discuss any situation, especially political and sexual ones'. Perls' assessment of how Reich worked: 'With him the importance of facts began to fade'. The interest in attitudes moved more into the foreground and foreshadowed the core conditions of Carl Rogers.

Reich (1969) emphasized understanding patients' forms of expression rather than the content of their speech. He believed that stories must be accompanied by the appropriate effect. Emotions were, he maintained, a manifestation of the flow of body energy. Unacceptable emotions were blocked and located in the tightening of the muscles; Reich referred to this process as 'muscular armouring', which can be seen as a chronic state of retroflection. Retroflection was defined by Perls *et al.* (1951) as the process of blocking some behaviour through opposing sensorimotor tensions. Conversely, relaxing these patterns of muscular armouring freed repressed emotions and blocked energy. He emphasized the expression of powerful feelings, and dealing with them in therapy. He stressed the non-verbal aspects of the client's behaviour as a means of increasing awareness of the body. Perls adopted this approach of Reich, and stressed body sensations as an avenue to awareness in gestalt therapy.

Reich (1969) believed that analysts should control the interaction with the patient. He held that there were three phases in interpreting resistances: analysts first interpreted that the patient was resisting; they then interpreted how this was occurring; and finally they interpreted what was being resisted. Confrontation was the method Reich advocated to eliminate resistance. Perls (1973) adopted the technique of confrontation but used it to frustrate the client. In 1989 he claimed that psychological growth happens only through frustration. His method was to confront those manipulations and neurotic patterns which supported the client's lack of responsibility. Naranjo (1980) sums up Reich's influence on Perls thus: 'From Reich he took his understanding of defense as a motor event and his recognition of the importance of expression' (p. 3).

Friedlander and gestalt therapy

The influence of Friedlander on gestalt therapy can be gauged by Perls' (1969a) words 'I recognise three gurus in my life. The first one was S. Friedlander, who called himself a Neo-Kantian. I learned from him the meaning of balance, the zero-centre of opposites'. It is interesting to note that his other two gurus were Selig, the sculptor and architect at the Esalen Institute, and Mitzie, a white cat!

In the early 1920s Perls was considerably influenced by the philosopher Friedlander and his ideas on differential thinking. Friedlander believed that whatever is, will polarize into opposites. If one is trapped by one of the opposing forces, then one acquires a one-sided outlook and one's life becomes out of balance. The balanced person, by comparison, stays in the homeostasis of the zero centre, like the eye of the hurricane. By remaining alert at the centre, a person can see both sides of an occurrence. Any departure from the zero-point is experienced as painful, the return as pleasurable.

Gestalt psychology and gestalt therapy

In 1926, Perls went to work at the Institute for Brain Damaged Soldiers with Kurt Goldstein, who emphasized the integral nature of the person. He demonstrated how injury to one part of the person acts not only on the affected part, but skews the entire range of the person's behaviours. Goldstein was a member of the gestalt school of psychology which dealt principally with perception and learning. Its founder was Max Wertheimer (1880–1943).

Wertheimer criticized Wundt for explaining sensory experiences in terms of elements, and believed that perception occurred in terms of wholes. He discovered that when a person perceived a vertical line, and 0.02 seconds later a horizontal line of the same length, the line seemed to fall from the vertical to the horizontal position to the perceiver. There was no evident point-to-point correspondence between stimulus and perception, since the line was static. There was a sense of motion without content, an experience Wertheimer referred to as a 'purephi phenomenon'. Individuals perceive their environment as a total unit of meaning. They respond to the whole of what they see, and this whole is composed of the stimuli to which they react and those to which they do not react. The person strives to integrate the two lines into a whole, since parts of anything have no meaning.

This principle was proposed by Ehrenfelds (1890, cited in Boring 1950). He stated that form in time and space is the sum of other qualities. An individual will view broken lines and construct from them the object they resemble. An example is that of a square formed from four lines. The whole is seen as defining the parts, in contrast with previous assumptions that the whole is merely the total sum of its parts. Heidbreder (1961) pointed out that a melody is a temporal form or pattern independent of the sensory elements of which it is composed. That is, the melody may be played in different keys, in different intensities, while still remaining the same melody.

The foregoing perceptions emphasize both the differentiation and the integration of figure and ground. Kurt Koffka (1887–1941), who assisted Wertheimer, who asserted that during the process of perception, figure and ground emerge. An exception exists where the visual field is undifferentiated, as in the case of a thick fog. What the person focuses on is the figure, while the ground is the context against which that figure appears. Gestalt psychology hypothesized that an object becomes the focus of the person's attention, and fades into the background as a different object from the background becomes figure. Thus figure and ground change as a new gestalt is formed.

Interruptions in the continuous flow of figure/ground interactions lead to an accumulation of incomplete gestalts. The gestalt psychologists postulated the principle of closure, whereby a person seeks to complete a figure and to perceive it as a whole. Zeigarnik, a student of Lewin's, applied this principle to unfinished tasks. She found that children recalled 2.5 times as many interrupted as completed tasks, while for adults the corresponding figure was 1.9. Another of Lewin's students, Orsiankina, involved nursery school children in such activities as cutting out paper patterns and moulding animals in clay. The children completed some of the activities, while others were interrupted without explanation. When free time was made available, 80% of the interrupted tasks were completed while far fewer of the completed tasks were pursued. Zeigarnik and Orsiankina based their experiments on Lewin's tension system hypothesis. He postulated that when one begins a task there is a high level of tension which is reduced when the task is completed; thus tension reduction was characterized as closure.

Existentialism and gestalt therapy

Perls was greatly influenced by existentialism in his development of gestalt therapy. Corey (1985) referred to gestalt therapy as 'a form of existential therapy' (p. 274). Perls (1969a) claimed that gestalt therapy was one of only three existential therapies, the other two being Frankl's logotherapy and Binswanger's *dasein* therapy. Foremost among the contributions provided by existentialism to gestalt therapy were the concepts of personal responsibility, the present moment, and awareness.

Existentialism stressed that individuals are responsible for their own existence. This influence can be seen in Perls' (1969b) definition of maturation as 'the transcendence from environmental to self-support' (p. 28). Although the existentialists stressed personal responsibility, Perls felt that they did not concretize their ideas. He stated, 'Existentialism wants to do away with concepts – the setback with the present existentialist philosophies is that they need their support from somewhere else. If you look at the existentialists, they say that they are non-conceptual, but if you look at the people they all borrow concepts from other sources. Buber from Judaism, Tillich from Protestantism, Sartre from Socialism, Heidegger from language, Binswanger from psychoanalysis'. Perls believed that individuals act on their environment by choosing what they do, what they feel and what they think. These decisions make individuals responsible human beings. Choice, however, is a function of the present.

Gestalt therapy rejected the traditional approach of existentialism. By considering the processes that underlie the experience, individuals discover how they live. Their perception of concrete events in the present constitutes their world. Kierkegaard (1944) emphasized that what individuals do in a real situation is what defines them. This has often been simplified as 'What is, is' or, behaviourally, by 'What you do is what you do'. Existentialists believe that things change by paying attention to them in the present moment. Smith (1977) states 'It is the living phenomenon which is of interest in gestalt therapy, the here-and-now phenomenon' (p. 17). Explaining current behaviour by means of past events leads only to explanations, speculations and interpretations which cover up or are removed from the original experience. What is important is to become aware of present behaviour and experiences.

SOUTH AFRICA: A TURNING POINT

Perls left Germany in 1933 and settled in Amsterdam, where he worked in private practice. In 1934, when he was sent to South Africa at the behest of Ernst Jones, President of the International Association of Psychoanalysis, (cf., Rosenfeld, 1978), he was still a firm believer in psychoanalysis. The following year Perls established the South African Institute for Psychoanalysis. In 1936 he presented a paper entitled 'Oral resistance' at the International Conference of Psychoanalysis in Czechoslovakia. At this congress he met Freud. Perls' words on the importance of such an event are revealing: referring to a year he spent in Vienna in 1927 he says, 'The Master was there, somewhere in the background. To meet him would have been too presumptuous. I had not yet earned such a privilege . . . In 1936 I thought I had. Was I not the mainspring for the creation of one of his institutes and did I not come 4000 miles to attend his congress'.

Perls (1969a) admits that he suffered disappointment and shock on what occurred at the visit. At the appointed time, Freud appeared in the doorway and remained there. Perls related the dual purpose of his visit from South Africa, namely, to present a paper and to see Freud. Freud's first question to Perls as related by Perls was 'When are you going back?'. Renate (cf. Shepard, 1976) states 'My father came back a very different man'. This encounter in the long term provided a freeing process for Perls. He allowed his unexpressed doubts about the Freudian system to emerge. It motivated him to seek the therapeutic approach in which he ultimately came to believe.

The beginning of gestalt therapy appeared in print 6 years later in his first book, *Ego, hunger and aggression*. Here he formulated what are now referred to as retroflection, introjection and projection. Although still couched in Freudian terminology, he affirmed taking responsibility for oneself and paying attention to the body.

THE BIRTH OF GESTALT THERAPY

In the summer of 1946, Perls moved to New York. He was followed in the autumn of 1947 by Laura and the children. He met Eric Fromm, who helped him to set up a flourishing practice. However, he was rejected by the Psychoanalytical Institute because of his use of his own personal approach to psychotherapy. He continued to experiment with his own ideas in his private practice, and in 1952, wrote his second book, *Gestalt Therapy*. This was co-authored by Ralph Hefferline and Paul Goodman. At the time, Hefferline was working as an assistant professor of psychology at Columbia University. He remained there, becoming chairman of the department in 1965, and died in 1974. Goodman is credited with writing the major part of the second half of the book and thus developing gestalt therapy into a coherent theory. As a result of this publication, the New York Institute of Gestalt Therapy was founded in the same year and located at 315 Central Park West.

It was during this New York period that the approach, for working in a group context, devised by the Perls and referred to as the 'hot seat', developed. Essentially one participant who volunteered to work became the focus of therapy, while the remaining group members were the audience for the work. These observed the process while engaging in their own self-therapy through identification with aspects of the ongoing work. Perls (1967) stated 'I carry the load of the session, by either doing individual therapy or by conducting mass experiments . . . I often interfere if the group plays opinion and interpretation games or has similar purely verbal encounters . . . A dyad is temporarily developed between myself and the patient, but the rest of the group is fully involved, though seldom as active participants. Mostly they act as an audience which is stimulated to do quite a bit of silent self-therapy' (p. 309). Group process *per se* was not given a great deal of attention. The most important reality was that of the client.

1954 saw the foundation of the Cleveland Institute for Gestalt Therapy in New York. Three people from Cleveland had attended a 10-day course with Fritz and Lore Perls. As a result, Fritz and Laura travelled frequently to Cleveland to conduct workshops. In 1956, he left Laura and went to Miami. From there he kept in touch with the gestalt groups in New York, Toronto, Cleveland and Detroit. In 1957, he met a 32-year-old woman named Marty Fromm whom he described in his autobiography as 'the most significant woman in my life'. During 1958, he spent a few months training psychiatric residents at the Psychiatric Clinic attached to Columbus (Ohio) State Hospital.

That same year he attended the American Psychological Association meeting in San Francisco, where he met Wilson van Dusen, author of *The natural depth in man*. Van Dusen was impressed with Perls 'because Fritz was seeing well beyond what everyone else had seen' (Shepard, 1976, p. 95). In 1959 he left for California and lived with the van Dusens for nearly 6 weeks. With van Dusen and Paul Frey, he worked at Mendocino State Hospital. He moved to Los Angeles in late 1960 where his friend and former student, Jim Simkin, helped him to set up a practice. In 1964, when he was almost 70 years old, he moved as consultant psychiatrist to the Esalen Institute in Big Sur, California. There he established a training group for therapists. It was during this period that he established himself as an innovator in psychotherapy.

Perls' time in Canada was short. In May 1969 he moved to Lake Cowichan on Vancouver Island, British Columbia, where he established a therapeutic community. Lamper (1971b) provides an interesting account of life there during the year following Perls' death. On Vancouver Island, Perls wrote the final pages of his autobiography *In and out of the garbage pail* (Perls, 1969a). He also completed transcripts of group therapy sessions which appeared in a book entitled *Gestalt therapy verbatim* (Perls, 1969b). In 1973, his book *The gestalt approach and eye witness to therapy* was published posthumously.

Having read Gaines' (1979) biography of Perls, Zinker (1979) concluded that Perls' daily life was 'not unlike the screwed up lives of many geniuses whose creative endeavours far outstripped their interpersonal dealings' (p. 27). Yet creativity alone was not his only gift, as reflected by Zinker's (1979) words: 'For me he was a master teacher' (p. 34). Perls died in March 1970. Van Dusen's (cf. Zinker, 1979) epitaph is a fitting conclusion: 'There went an immensely gifted man' (p. 33).

Chapter 2

Gestalt-related concepts, goals and processes

Chapter 1 touched briefly on some of the concepts related to gestalt therapy. We now examine these and other gestalt-related concepts in greater depth.

GESTALT-RELATED CONCEPTS

Gestalt

The word 'gestalt' has no adequate English equivalent. Many terms have been suggested, such as form, structure, configuration, but the closest approximation is the word 'whole'. Gestalt therapists hold that a response to a situation must be 'whole', involving the totality of the person. An analysis of the different parts of an individual cannot provide an understanding of the whole. The whole is defined and exists only by virtue of the interrelation of the parts.

In forming a gestalt we give meaning to what is happening to us. For example, if I want to discover my particular reaction to my home life, I determine the aspects of the situation which please or displease me. This leads me to a better personal understanding of the implications of the situation. Even if I decide to change nothing, I still have a better awareness of who I am in family life. If I opt to make some alterations, I have a greater understanding of what form these might take. If what I discover is distasteful to me, I am clear what aspects I am unhappy with. I acquire a sense of possibility for change. Perls (1973) suggested that any aspect of a person's behaviour could be regarded as a manifestation of the whole. In this way, what individuals do provides as much information as what they feel, think or say. The human being is thus a unit consisting of many parts which function interrelatedly. Through gestalt therapy the person may become fully functioning and self-supportive, and form a complete gestalt conducive to growth and psychological health.

Figure and ground

When a person's experiences form a meaningful whole, healthy function-ing exists. A smooth transition results when certain happenings are in the focus of awareness, while others are in the background. As I write I become aware that my car is parked in an area which is a no-parking zone after 9.00 a.m. It is now 10.45 a.m. As I continue to write, the need to move the car becomes more persistent, so that it is more difficult to concentrate. I move the car.

This situation illustrates the figure/ground dichotomy of gestalt therapy. At first the figure, which is the important object of awareness, was the expression of my thoughts on paper. The ground, or background, included the street where my car was parked. As my awareness moved to the car, writing was no longer of primary importance as the car became the figure of my interest. When I moved the car I was psychologically free to return to my work. Within a few minutes, writing alternated between being figure, ground and then figure again. Healthy functioning requires this fluidity of process. Inability to move my figure while writing could have resulted in an undesirable fine. A premise underlying the figure/ground principle is that the individual must be able to differentiate between the more promin-ent and less prominent stimuli in the surroundings at any given time. One must be flexible in one's interaction with the environment.

Through contacting inner experience, the individual becomes aware of a demand which emerges as foreground/figure against the background of his/her total personality. For example, when a person is hungry, food is essential. Once this need is satisfied, it merges into the ground until another becomes dominant. In this way interest and need determine figure.

At any given time there may be several demands clamouring for atten-tion; that which is most important to the person's survival or self-actualization will become the figure. In healthy functioning the individual clearly differentiates this dominant need. As it increases, excitement is generated, activating the person to satisfy it. The figure then merges into the background, and the next most important need becomes the new figure. Thus different figures continuously emerge and recede.

In neurotic individuals the relationship between themselves and their environment is such that they cannot satisfy any emerging dominant need. No one demand becomes figure against the background. When figures remain dull, confused or lacking in energy, either something in the environment is being blocked out or some need of the individual is not being expressed. Sahakian (1976) states that in this instance individuals are not 'all there', i.e. their whole field cannot lend its resources to the completion of the figure.

Rubin (cited in Woodworth and Schlosberg, 1954) gives five major differences between figure and ground:

1. The figure has form, while the ground tends to be formless.
2. The ground appears to extend continuously behind the figure without being interrupted by it.
3. The figure has a quality of 'thingness', while the ground has a quality of undifferentiated material.
4. The figure appears nearer than the ground.
5. It is the figure rather than the ground which is more impressive, better remembered, and more apt to be given meaning.

Balance

Perls (1969b) believed that the healthy individual operates within an appropriate balance of all parts. This balance must be maintained within certain limits for survival; this is the principle of homeostasis. There is an inherent drive within individuals to maintain this equilibrium in order to grow and develop to their full potential: people do this by accepting the feelings and experiences arising within them.

At every moment the person is faced with dissonance, either through an external demand or through an internal need, so that balance is never maintained. In relation to external factors, the individual can choose to accommodate behaviour to the environment, or to adjust the environment to himself. Perls (1969b) pointed out that the human being regains equilibrium through gratifying or eliminating these needs and demands, and referred to this process as 'organismic self-regulation'. By using this approach, he claimed that he was doing away with the whole instinct theory of Freud.

This balance is something which must be attained in an atmosphere full of splits. We tend to see life in terms of contrasts rather than balance. For example, we think of strong as being the opposite of gentle. We rarely integrate them and speak in terms of being gently strong or strongly gentle. In gestalt therapy, whenever we recognize one aspect of ourselves, the presence of its opposite is implicit. While 'being gentle' is in our foreground, we experience it against the background of 'being strong'. In this manner we can speak of being strongly gentle and achieve equilibrium. The emphasis is on integrating the two parts so that whichever is appropriate may surface in a given situation. Thus individuals allow themselves to be either gentle or strong, depending on the situation in which they are. Integration of the two frees them from the feeling that they must be either strong or gentle, when an appropriate reaction depends on both.

A well known polarity identified by Perls, Hefferline and Goodman (1951) is that of the top dog/underdog. The top dog is authoritarian, parental and judgemental, while the underdog is submissive and apologetic. Since we cannot lead a whole life without both of these aspects of ourselves, gestalt therapy works towards an integration of the two, where neither will dominate but where a balance of both is effectively achieved.

Awareness

Perls (1969b) believed that individuals should be capable of becoming fully aware of and acting upon their needs. He stated that 'awareness is the only basis of knowledge and communication' (p. 48). It is the process of recognizing what we are thinking about and what we are feeling, sensing and doing. It may be viewed from different perspectives. Perls (1969b) differentiated between three zones: 'awareness of self, awareness of the world, and awareness of what is between'.

Awareness is not introspection: in introspection, the self is both subject and object; the self is both 'I' and 'me'. James (1890) distinguished between these two aspects: the 'I' is the self as observer and knower; the 'me' is the self as observed, as an object. In introspection, the 'I' observes the 'me'. The self is split; it looks at itself self-consciously. Perls (1969b) compares awareness to the glow of a coal which comes from its own combustion, and introspection to the light reflected from an object when a flashlight is turned on it.

Awareness involves the total self focusing on the figure. It is not concerned with the unconscious but with the obvious, the surface. It starts with what is, and growth occurs through this. In gestalt therapy it does not refer to the generally accepted significance of the word, which usually relates to content or a thought about a problem; rather, it focuses on a deeper insight. The therapist seeks to catalyse awareness in clients until they awaken to their responsibility for thinking, feeling and acting.

Perls (1969b) believed that awareness is curative. Its development is linked to the growing knowledge of the client. This understanding is based on how individuals prevent themselves from experiencing, feeling or acting. The task of the therapist, according to O'Leary and Martin (1989), is to catalyse awareness in clients by confronting the actual situation in the present moment. Clients are encouraged to pay attention to their process and to the what and how of such observations. Focusing on what they are feeling in the current situation leads to an increased consciousness of the present. By attending to moment-to-moment changes they discover how they are functioning in the world.

Awareness focuses on the obvious. It concentrates on the client's movements, postures, language patterns, voice, gestures and interactions. Perls

(1969b) believed that many people fail to use their senses properly; the gestalt therapist invites clients to do this, to become aware of how they avoid the obvious and to open themselves to what is here now. Polster and Polster (1973) state that 'at its best, awareness is a continuous means for keeping up to date with one's self ... It is always there, like an underground stream, ready to be tapped into when needed, a refreshing and revitalizing experience' (p. 211).

Increasing awareness is the therapeutic core of gestalt therapy. This development relates to experience rather than to intellectualization. Any present situation can be contacted, felt and described, rather than explained and interpreted. Kempler (1974) states that present awareness influences subsequent awareness as psychological processes roll on the wheel of awareness–experience–awareness. In this way individuals perceive life as it is right now, and are able to deal with all aspects of this realization. Thoughts, actions, feelings, the manner in which people live, are all in harmony with the way they feel. Life ceases to be a pretence, as individuals act the way they really are. They are what people see.

Fagan and Shepherd (1970) believe that for healing to occur, individuals must comprehend their uniqueness and find ways of expressing it. The therapist enables them to appreciate the internal resources they possess to solve their problems. Enright (1970) points out that the experience of increased awareness is frequently accompanied by a release of tension that is pleasurable, even if the realization is of a painful situation. In this manner, awareness is linked with the growing knowledge and understanding of how one represses or avoids disagreeable memories or experiences – 'unfinished business' as it is called in gestalt therapy.

Unfinished business

The term 'unfinished business' was derived by Perls, Hefferline and Goodman (1951) from the gestalt psychology principle of closure. When we perceive a figure that is incomplete, the mind acts to perfect it and to view it as ended. Perls extended this principle to therapy. Incomplete experiences and feelings persist in the memory of the perceiver. It is a tendency of the organism to conclude any situation or transaction that is unfinished. Polster and Polster (1973) agree with this position; they state 'These incomplete directions do seek completion and when they get powerful enough, the individual is beset with preoccupation, compulsive behaviour, wariness, oppressive energy and much self-defeating behaviour' (p. 36).

Unfinished business, according to Hatcher and Himelstein (1976), refers to the blocking of an emotion that was experienced at one or more times during a relationship. Instead of allowing themselves to experience the feelings which accompanied traumatic events, individuals with unfinished business inhibit them. The termination of a relationship through sudden death, divorce or separation often results in unfinished business. In these instances, individuals either did not grieve or avoided finishing the relationship and saying goodbye. They ignored their unpleasant feelings, which then went underground. This resulted in unresolved feelings or unfulfilled needs.

Unfinished business does not relate solely to relationships which have terminated. When physical distance exists between two people who are in a relationship, unfinished business between them will often come to the foreground. It is as if, irrespective of distance, each situation looks for closure: it clamours for attention. Therefore, some time apart can be enriching for two people in a relationship, as it enables both of them to find separately any unfinished business in that relationship. Certain behaviours are indicative of incomplete situations, e.g. wallowing in self-pity, whining or nagging. Berne (1967) is really speaking of unfinished business in a person's life when he speaks of games such as 'Poor little me', and 'If it weren't for you'. Since much of depression is closely connected to these, the depressed person is another example of someone who is suffering from unfinished business.

Unfinished business saps the person of the necessary motivation to engage in other activities. It obscures present experience and hinders the investment of energy in current events. As Goulding and Goulding (1979) state, 'clients who do not say goodbye keep a part of their energy locked in yesterdays' (p. 175). Individuals with unfinished business are, in fact, unwilling to experience the pain that they feel and move forward. To do so would involve changing feelings, thoughts and perceptions. The unfinished situation serves as an excuse for not getting involved. Sometimes the person experiences conflict with regard to letting the other go. A man/woman who has experienced a happy marriage and whose spouse is now dead often feels a sense of betrayal in considering entering into a new relationship. Attitudes of family, friends or culture can augment this.

Avoidance is the means individuals use to prevent themselves from completing unfinished business. Perls (1969b) thought that most people choose to shun painful emotions than to do what is necessary to change. They then become stuck, blocking their possibilities of growth. Working with these blocks is both difficult and painful. Perls, Hefferline and Goodman (1951) point out that avoidance exists for good and sufficient reasons, and hence the task is to become aware of the reasons for its existence.

Repetition is a sign that a situation unfinished in the past is still incomplete in the present. Each reoccurrence aims at a solution; what makes the attempt unsuccessful is the fixed attitude which accompanies it and which prevents completion. The unfinished situation continues to press for attention, thus setting up a spiral leading from figure to repression and returning to figure. In this manner, individuals do not look for incomplete situations. They form the focus of their attention spontaneously.

Enright (1970) saw unfinished business as leading to the blocking of awareness and interfering with the completion of need cycles. It leads to an arousal in tension, but not to the expression effect. Cohn (1970) equates unfinished business with emotional fixation. She states that the difference between these terms is that fixation expresses the deterministic philosophy of cause-and-effect oriented thinking. Unfinished business, however, belongs to a philosophy that challenges individuals to take responsibility for whatever they are. Perls (1970) describes fixated people as those who hang on doggedly, and will not let go. They cling to exhausted relationships from which they no longer get any profit. They hold on to outworn customs, to memories, to grudges. They will not try a new adventure. As they are enabled to let go of their blocks, tension is released and feelings that were hitherto buried, are voiced. This is usually accompanied by a freeing of energy.

Resentments figure prominently in unfinished business. Perls (1970) felt that they were the most common and important forms of unfinished business, relating to demands that have not been made explicit. Passons (1975) describes them as the bulldogs of unexpressed feelings, in terms of retaining their bite: anger that should be voiced is hoarded within the person. Perls, Hefferline and Goodman (1951) refer to the guilty and the resentful as 'clingers' – they hang on. Whereas guilt is the self-punitive vindictive attitude towards oneself, resentment is the demand that the other person feel guilt; both avoid finishing a situation. Perls (1969b) said, 'Whenever you feel guilty, find out what you are resenting and express it, and make your demands explicit' (p. 53).

Kubler-Ross (1984) sheds further light on unfinished business when she distinguishes between grief and grief work. Grief, she holds, is a very natural emotion which involves shedding tears, sharing and talking. It is not necessary to work with it. Grief work, on the other hand, involves shame, guilt and fear. An alternative conceptualization of this is Glasser's (1984) distinction of 'pure feeling' and 'long-term feeling behaviours'. Pure feelings, he believes, refer to the 'immediate, usually intense, short-term feeling, which occurs at the moment of frustration or satisfaction'. Long-term feeling behaviours, on the other hand, are chosen to prolong the satisfaction. Glasser, then, would view grief as pure feeling, but grief work as relating to long-term feeling behaviours.

Present-centredness

Gestalt therapy fosters a 'here-and-now' orientation. Staying with the immediate moment is of paramount importance in the client's attempt to achieve genuine awareness. The present alone is of significance, for the past is gone and the future has not yet arrived; the past and future are significant only when they are rooted in the now. It is not the content of childhood memories that is important, but the feelings or attitudes surrounding them. When people think of the future they anticipate what is to come: energy can be invested which bears little relation to what eventually emerges. Whatever is actual, according to Perls (1969b), is always in the present.

Perls (1973) considered gestalt to be an experiential therapy rather than just a verbal one. If individuals think and talk about a situation, they interrupt the flow of present-centredness and become detached from themselves. Thinking and talking about an experience is known as 'about-ism'. The power of the present resides in the ongoing awareness of each consecutive moment. The 'now' does not exist simply as one instant in time, but rather it relates to a stream of consciousness formed by a series of nows, like the succession of frames in a film. The gestalt therapist seeks to increase the client's awareness of what they are feeling from moment to moment. Polster and Polster (1973) state that 'A most difficult truth to teach is that only the present exists now, and to stray from it distracts from the living quality of reality' (p. 7).

Self-criticism, blame, guilt, judgements relating to self or others, can prevent individuals from becoming involved with themselves or with others in the present. Many people find they need to criticize those around them in order to avoid considering their own experience. Others blank out their now when they have time to reflect on what is happening. Growth will only occur when they open themselves to the possibility of considering the now.

Responsibility for oneself

Being responsible for oneself is at the core of gestalt therapy. Clients are assisted to move from a position of dependence on others, including the therapist, to a state of being self-supporting. They are encouraged to do many things independently. Initially they see their feelings, emotions and problems as being somehow outside themselves: they use phrases such as 'he makes me mad'. They assume no responsibility for what they are, and it seems to them that there is nothing they can do about their situation other than to accept it. They do not see themselves as having input into or control of their lives. Clients are helped to realize that they are responsible for what happens to them. It is they who must decide whether to change their life situation or allow it to remain unaltered.

Perls (1969b) maintains that we tend to cling to our past in order to justify our unwillingness to assume responsibility for the present. By remaining in the past, we can play endless games of blame for the way we are. We never really face our own capacity to move in new directions. We get caught up in the process of making resolutions about and rationalizing our lifeless state. We would rather do anything than become conscious of how we keep ourselves from being fully alive.

Contact

The significance of contact demands separate treatment, and will be dealt with in Chapter 3.

GOALS

The principal objectives of gestalt therapy are eliciting personal responsibility and achieving self-regulation. Perls (1969b) stated that the aim of therapy is to enable individuals to be aware *ab initio* of their own potential for independence. They can do many more things than they believed they could. They need no longer lead their lives according to the expectation of others, nor from unassimilated directives received in youth from parents or teachers: they effectively regulate themselves.

Self-regulation is possible when individuals identify themselves as growing and changing – it means that they now recognize themselves as they are and not as they would wish to be. They are free of unfinished business and are not burdened by the expectations of the future.

PROCESS

Process relates to movement and change. Perls (1970) compared the unfolding of adult personality to the peeling of an onion. Growing awareness assists the individual to progress through five layers of functioning, generally accepted as being: (1) the cliché or phoney, (2) the role-playing or phobic, (3) the impasse, (4) the implosive, and (5) the explosive. It is worthy of note, however, that Perls (1975) gave a different order to these layers, speaking first of the role-playing layer, then the implosive layer leading to the impasse, then the explosive layer and finally authentic living. The resulting confusion which ensued may explain why this area has been dealt with only partially or ignored in many books and chapters dealing with gestalt therapy (e.g. Polster and Polster, 1973; Sahakian, 1976).

The cliché or phoney layer, consists of shallow, token contact such as 'Good morning, How are you? Nice day isn't it?' By engaging in reflexive behaviour, people avoid communicating with themselves or with others. In the role-playing or phobic layer, people play roles rather than contact their true selves e.g. the efficient secretary, the capable businessman, the learned professor, the good little boy/girl, the devoted son/daughter, the diligent student, the model religious superior. These roles have usually emerged from the self-ideal. People pretend to be what they would like to be. Acting in this manner enables individuals to avoid considering what they dislike about themselves. They wrongly assume that others like them for what they pretend to be, rather than for what they are. They try to live up to the expectations of others. Games, as elucidated by Berne (1967), also occur in this layer. The roles and games are efforts to avoid the emotional pain that would occur if they were permitted into awareness. This blocking happens because individuals fear that they will be rejected by others. Hence poor self-esteem is the underlying root of role playing.

In the impasse, people stop playing games and roles; this often results in a feeling of not knowing what to do next. Van de Riet, Korb and Gorrell (1988) state that the impasse is reached when clients avoid working beyond a certain point. This is not a conscious manipulative behaviour: individuals are confronted by a vacuum or emptiness, and become stuck in their own maturation or growth. Patterson (1973) points out that the impasse has no basis in reality since the necessary resources exist to deal with the situation. People prevent themselves from using them through fear or catastrophic expectations. Perls, Hefferline and Goodman (1951) assert that in the impasse individuals give up their own eyes and ears, and try to manipulate others into doing their seeing and hearing for them. The impasse, then, is a function of the fantasy in which the person engages. It can be associated with a feeling of panic, as people struggle with the doubt that they have not the necessary resources to survive without role playing.

In any impasse opposing feelings and needs conflict as the problem works internally. Individuals allow themselves to become aware of these contradictions, and there may be an attempt to obtain environmental help by asking others to validate the previous roles or games. The impasse is the point where this aid stops and authentic self-support has yet to be generated. There is a loosening of the impasse when people discover that previously unacceptable behaviour brings unexpected satisfaction. The following dialogue which takes place between Tony, a young man, and Fritz Perls illustrates this impasse. In this filmed interview Tony is sitting in the chair next to Perls. Neither of them speaks for several minutes. Finally Perls calls to another member of the group:

Perls: 'Dick, did you not tell me Tony wanted to work on a dream?'
Tony: (Haltingly) 'I recently had a dream in which ... I had an opportunity to go abroad. I have never been out of New York. I have never been to Europe ... and I had an opportunity to go to Europe and I was going to fly from New York but I had to get a flight from my home in Ohio ...'
Perls: 'Please tell it in the present tense.'
Tony: 'OK, I have got to go to New York.'
Perls: 'What is your left foot doing?'
Tony: 'Bracing against that little stool.'
Perls: 'Close your eyes and enter your body. Describe what you feel physically.'
Tony: 'Fear ... Physically, I am warm. I am breathing hard and my heart is pounding ...'
Perls: 'What kind of voice do you use?'
Tony: 'It is more sure than it actually is ... It is affected.'
Perls: 'Well, you see it is clear that he is much too preoccupied with the stage fright to be ready to really work on the dream. We will do some actual work first. Now, can you look at the audience? What do you experience there?'
Tony: (Silently looking around the room) 'I ... feel better. I experience ... sort of a patience and I think they have a ...'
Perls: 'Close your eyes and withdraw again. Any place you would like to go. Where would you go?'
Tony: 'Do you mean in my body?'
Perls: 'Where you would feel more comfortable, away from us; your body, your fantasy, I do not know, just go away.'
Tony: 'I am out on one of the rocks out in the ocean.'
Perls: 'What are you doing there?'
Tony: 'I am looking back at Esalen, at the grounds.'
Perls: 'Are you all by yourself there?'
Tony: 'Yes.'
Perls: 'How does it feel to be by yourself?'
Tony: 'Well, I feel secure in the fact that I am out here ... and yet I feel incomplete in that I should be back on the ground ... encountering people.'
Perls: 'OK, open your eyes and encounter people.'
Tony: (He pauses for a long time as he looks at the members of the group).
Perls: 'What do you experience?'
Tony: 'Again I experience a patience and sort of a calm ... and ... uh ... a good feeling ... a rapport.'

Perls:	'A good feeling. I see your right hand doing this.' (Tony's right hand is clutching his right knee). 'What does this mean? How do you experience this?'
Tony:	'As tension.'
Perls:	'What kind of tension? May I interpret it? May I make a mistake? It looks to me like pushing away. OK, now close your eyes again and withdraw into your dream. What do you see, feel and hear? I do not want a story, I just want to see what you encounter when you go into your dream.'
Tony:	'Shame.'
Perls:	'Yeah, what are you ashamed of?'
Tony:	'. . . Of not accomplishing . . . trivial little things.'
Perls:	'Such as . . .?'
Tony:	'I . . . uh . . . I wasted just enough time so that I missed the airplane . . . and the opportunity to go to Europe. I . . .'
Perls:	'Have you ever been to Europe?'
Tony:	'No.'
Perls:	'Keep your eyes closed. Go to Europe, whatever Europe means to you. Go to Europe. What happens? Take the plane. I do not let you miss the plane. I put you on the plane.'
Tony:	'Uh, Uh . . . new people. A lot of people I do not know and they do not know me . . . uh, fresh personalities that . . . I mean . . . that . . . they are all in need.'
Perls:	'For this you have to go to Europe.'
Tony:	(Sighing) 'I do not know if it is my exact motivation . . . that is what I am seeking when I get there. That is one of the first things I experience . . .'
Perls:	'OK, now I put you back on the plane again. The plane lands in Monterey and I put you on a helicopter down to Esalen – you walk up to Fritz's room and open your eyes and what happens here? Open your eyes.'
Tony:	(Pausing for several minutes) 'I want to ask you what it is that you would imagine that I would imagine that I would do . . . I am not . . . sort of what you would expect.'
Perls:	'OK, produce a few expectations.'
Tony:	'Sir?'
Perls:	'Produce a few expectations.' (Tony sits in Dr. Perls' "empty chair" and they sit in silence for several minutes). 'Please do not change your posture. What is your right hand and left hand doing? How are they relating to each other?'
Tony:	(Tony is pounding his right fist into his cupped left hand). 'It is an encounter . . . tension.'

Perls:	'Can you sit here and keep the posture?' (Dr. Perls motions for Tony to return to his seat which he does and cups his right hand in his left). 'What does the right hand say and what does the left hand say?'
Tony:	'The left hand is stopping the right hand from moving . . . but the right hand has a grip, or has a catch – is holding the left hand.'
Perls:	'Give them the words. "I stop you". "I hold on to you". Make a Punch and Judy show out of it. Make it like puppets talking to each other.'
Tony:	'The left hand is saying, "Stop".'
Perls:	'Say it again.'
Tony:	'Stop!'
Perls:	'Again.'
Tony:	'Stop!'
Perls:	'Again.'
Tony:	'Stop!'
Perls:	'Louder.'
Tony:	'Stop!'
Perls:	'Louder.'
Tony:	'Stop!'
Perls:	'What does the right hand say?'
Tony:	(He sits silently for several seconds) 'The right hand is not going anywhere but it does not care because . . .'
Perls:	'Now, say I do not care.'
Tony:	'I do not care.'
Perls:	'Again.'
Tony:	'. . . I do not care.'
Perls:	'Again.'
Tony:	'I do not care.'
Perls:	'Again.'
Tony:	'I do not care.'
Perls:	'OK, now go into the dialogue.'
Tony:	'. . . You must stop pushing – No I do not – Stop pushing immediately!'

(The film pauses at this moment to allow the camera to be reloaded. During this period, Tony completes the dialogue between the left and right hands, a conversation that ends in an impasse. Dr. Perls directs Tony's attention to the group. The film resumes).

Tony:	(Tony surveys the group quietly). 'It is not a fear, but I sense that other people are . . . sort of gaining an insight . . . possibly to me . . .'

Perls: 'Other people gain insight, but you do not. It is still there – other people.'

Tony: 'Yes . . . I am starting to formulate something . . .'

Perls: 'I know, but do not force yourself.'

'Well, there is one thing that I want to point out that you might have noticed. Tony is an example of the implosive layer. There is an implosion here. (Fritz illustrates this layer by re-enacting Tony's hand dialogue). He is paralysing himself – both sides are exerting equal pressure so that the result is like a tug of war with no side winning. This is how he keeps himself in this fit of near-paralysis. He has to separate the parts and let them mobilize themselves separately. (Turning to Tony and shaking hands) OK?'

In the above example, the impasse is clearly illustrated in Tony's work with his right and left hands. This is particularly evident when he says 'The left hand is stopping the right hand from moving . . . but the right hand has a grip, or has a catch – is holding the left hand'. The impasse is further illustrated in Tony's attempt to get Perls to do his thinking for him: 'I want to ask you what it is that you would imagine that I would do . . . I am not . . . sort of what you would expect'.

An example of Tony's inauthentic mode of living can be seen when Perls directs his attention to the group. Rather than responding from an 'I' position, Tony voices what he feels the other group members are doing with respect to him. Tony's dependence on environmental support is highlighted when he says 'I sense that other people are . . . sort of gaining an insight . . . possibly to me . . .'. Perls responds: 'Other people gain insight, but you do not. It is still there – other people', to which Tony replies 'Yes'.

Van de Riet, Korb and Gorrell (1988) point out that the therapist, having worked with clients towards the recognition and removal of prior environmental manipulations for support, can help them discover a route through the impasse by helping them to support themselves. For growth to occur it is essential that people stay with the void in order to get through the impasse. Tobin (1975) claims that clients who avoid emptiness and loneliness try to hold the therapist's attention by chattering.

The impasse can be resolved in different ways, for example, by an experiment or confrontation. Polster and Polster (1973) state that a reshuffling of the familiar ingredients can impel individuals to move beyond a stale rehash of old contradictions. The therapist must aid clients to see how they block themselves, and how they create barriers to using their potential. This often results in frustration, which Perls (1969b) considered to be a necessary ingredient for growth. He recommended that therapists apply enough skilful frustration so that clients are forced to find their own way, to discover that what they expect from the therapist they can do just as well themselves.

The main function of the therapist at the point of impasse is to keep clients in touch with themselves. When they withdraw into intellectualizations, the therapist invites them to make 'I' statements. Individuals usually need assistance to live with the pain before they realize that it is tolerable. Van de Riet, Korb and Gorrell (1988) state: 'At the impasse, the most obvious (and often the simplest) configuration or movement is most serious and important . . . Since the client is unaware of the obvious, the therapist has to be aware of it' (p. 103).

Perls (1975) doubted that it was possible to work through the impasse in individual therapy, but felt that it was feasible to do so when an integration of individual and group therapy occurred. In individual therapy it is relatively easy for the client to dismiss the observations of the therapist, whereas in group therapy the collective responses of group members make this less likely. Perls states in this regard: 'Somehow trust in the group seems to be greater than trust in the therapist' (p. 12).

The implosive layer is characterized by fear. Perls (1975) believed that Freud mistook this for the death instinct, whereas in fact the rigidity associated with it comes about through the existence of two equally strong forces residing within the individual. In the following example these two forces are represented by the client, Denis, and his mother. The therapist has invited Denis to use the empty chair to set up a dialogue between his mother and himself. At the beginning of the session Denis had described his mother's expectation that he would be a good student.

Denis: 'I remember the time that I came back with an 'S' in writing. I think that was while I was in fourth grade. You went to the teacher to get it corrected to an 'E' because I had good writing and you were outraged that she had given me an 'S' which meant satisfactory.'

Mother: 'Well I had to do that. She had no business giving you an 'S'. When I asked her about it she said that she gave you satisfactory because she chose to mark students on improvement and your writing was already so good that it could not improve. Well I was not going to stand for that. I went right up to the principal and he agreed with me. He made the teacher speak to me and ultimately she changed the grade to an 'E'.'

Denis: 'The whole thing embarrassed me. I could not see what difference it made.'

Mother: 'That was your record. That is how people see how you performed.'

Denis:	'I was not interested in an 'E'. I wanted to play baseball and ride my pony.'
Mother:	'That was my responsibility as a parent. I am a teacher and I know that these things count.'
Denis:	'Who do they count for? Who besides Daddy and you are ever going to look at my 'S'? What difference does it make?'
Mother:	'That is not the point. You are one of the best writers in the class. I did the school a service. The teacher said that she appreciated my point of view. It all worked out very well.'
Denis:	'I have got other things to do. I am going to play baseball.'
Therapist:	'What are you feeling?'
Denis:	'My feeling is absurd.'
Therapist:	'Absurd?'
Denis:	'She is focusing on something and making a big issue out of it.'
Therapist:	'And your feeling?'
Denis:	'The feeling place is in my stomach.'
Therapist:	'In your stomach?'
Denis:	'Yes down there.'
Therapist:	'Are you feeling it right now?'
Denis:	'Not now but I was feeling it then.'

Denis relates two embarrassing incidents: the first was the teacher's visit to his home in relation to his grade for writing; the second was when as a young lad he was teased by a girl in the choir, which was predominantly female. His mother's intervention in the problem embarrassed him greatly. The therapist invites the adult Denis to tell his mother (through the use of the empty chair) how he feels.

Denis:	'When the teacher came to the house I was embarrassed. I thought she should not have given me the 'S'. I did not like that but it also seemed a big deal was being made out of it.'
Therapist:	'As an adult what would you like to say to your mother?'
Denis:	'You do not have to be that precise and you do not have to make a big deal out of small issues. Who you are is a lot more important than what the world is giving you.'
Therapist:	'Getting it right in front of the world is not that important?'
Denis:	'Doing the best you can is important but how the world measures you is secondary and it is good to keep those two things in mind and not get confused about which one is the most important.'
Therapist:	'What does your mother say to that?'
Mother:	'Look at my 80th birthday. All those people came. It is true

	that Jean arranged it. She did call people to ask them to stop by. She understood how important it was to me. That is what kept me going.'
Denis:	'It did keep you going and I am glad it worked for you. I do not want to do what you did.'
Therapist:	'Tell her exactly what you do not want to do.'
Denis:	'I do not want to put energy in superficial things. I want to focus on how I am relating to people and attend to spiritual things.'
Therapist:	'What does she say to that?'
Mother:	'You know that I agree with that. I always wanted you to be happy and that is my view too.'
Denis:	'You say that that is your view but as I looked at the way you lived your life, the things you made the biggest issue about, it seems to me that the way people reacted to you was the biggest issue for you.'
Mother:	'It is important how people respond to you and who they think you are. The things I used to do gave people a lot of pleasure. They felt good about being invited to my parties and they told me repeatedly how nice it was for them.'
Denis:	'I am glad for you that it worked and I do not want to do the same thing.'
Therapist:	'Tell her exactly what you are going to do.'
Denis:	'I am going to put my energy into my own spiritual development and inner growth.'
Therapist:	'What does she say?'
Mother:	'You were always pretty independent. It does not surprise me that you are going to do things differently to me. Just remember there are a lot of people around you and you have to take them into account.'
Denis:	'That is true. I try to do that and I am having some difficulty. Sarah dislikes my emphasis on preciseness. I believe that it is rooted in my childhood.'
Mother:	'It certainly does not have anything to do with what happened in our household. What you got there was a lot of love and support.'
Denis:	'That is true and I also got a lot of expectations and a lot of guilt if they were not met.'
Mother:	'I never made you guilty.'
Denis:	'When I used to ring you, you used to say "I bet you broke your arm. We have not got a letter in two months".'
Mother:	'That was just a joke. Can you not take a joke?'

Denis:	'You said that it was a joke but the reality was that you were trying to punish me or make me conform to what you wanted to happen.'
Mother:	'It certainly was not too much to expect you to write a letter once in a while.'
Denis:	'The reality is that I wrote as many letters as you did. No matter what I did it was never quite good enough. When I used to visit you used to start to cry when I was leaving.'
Therapist:	'That was because I loved you so much. My family was everything to me.'
Denis:	'That was the problem. If I did not live up to your expectations you were hurt and you conveyed that hurt to me.'
Mother:	'I certainly was not trying to hurt you. I loved you so much. You have no idea until you have children of your own. You have no idea how important they are.'
Denis:	'I have children and I do know how important they are. I am trying to act differently with them. I feel good about it.'
Mother:	'Well you have wonderful children and I am glad that you are happy.'

At this point Denis exclaims 'I feel finished'. The therapist invites him to look at his mother and check how he feels. The session concludes as follows:

Denis:	'When you died in my arms two years ago, I felt that we had come to a conclusion but maybe those pieces were not complete. I feel better now.'
Therapist:	'See how she feels.'
Mother:	'When I died I felt that my life was complete and I feel that we have come to an even better understanding now.'

The equality of the two forces is very evident in the above example. Both express their own feelings very strongly, which allows interaction between the two parts. Movement into the explosive layer is heralded as Denis asserts 'Who you are is a lot more important than what the world is giving you'.

The explosive layer is the prelude to authentic living. It can be equated with the moment of insight for clients where the scales fall from their eyes. It is what Powell (1976) refers to as being fully human, fully alive. Individuals rediscover their lost emotions, and psychological energy is restored. The deadness of the impasse phase is replaced by a feeling of aliveness. Explosions can vary in intensity from slight tremblings to experiences that fully involve the body. Perls (1975) differentiates between four areas of explosion: sexual love, anger, joy and grief. Grief, since it is socially acceptable, is often the easiest to reach. Anger and sexual love receive the most attention, although explosion into sexual love, Perls believed, is often difficult. The neurotic finds the greatest difficulty with joy.

Chapter 3

Contact

Contact is at the heart of gestalt therapy. Perls, Hefferline and Goodman (1951) acknowledged its importance but did not develop it adequately. Rosenblatt (1980) emphasized its significance when he stated that what therapists need to rely on is not their technique but their personal development and the quality of their contact with clients, but the groundwork had already been laid by Polster and Polster (1973). They stressed the importance of a selective exchange between people and their setting. The meeting place of individuals and their surroundings is called a contact boundary. The state of this boundary was, in Perls, Hefferline and Goodman's (1951) opinion, an indication of the relationship between the two. In a healthy individual it is flexible and the person is fully engaged in the process of interacting with the environment.

As material is assimilated boundaries can be extended and the capacity of individuals for contacting, organizing, breaking down and assimilating larger aspects of the environment are made possible. This growth is continuous, dynamic and ongoing. Healthy human beings know that they are separate and can risk union without losing awareness of internal and external conditions. Not so the unhealthy, such as the neurotic who may fear loss of self through contact. For them, the boundary between the person and the environment is disturbed. Distressed human beings allow fewer opportunities for contact to happen; they maintain fixed behaviours and perceptions when faced with potentially exciting but threatening possibilities from interaction. Energy is turned back towards the self. They attempt to satisfy needs without including the environmental other. Assimilation is prevented and integration does not occur. The individual is, as it were, encapsulated.

Polster and Polster (1973) identify five different types of contact boundary: body boundaries, value boundaries, familiarity boundaries, expressive boundaries and exposure boundaries. The nature of the body boundary varies from person to person: some individuals experience no sensation below the neck – they function solely from a cognitive view of the world. Others sense their emotions (e.g. fear) in their stomach, but have no awareness of their pelvic area or the sexual dimension of their living. By paying attention to breathing, those areas of the body of which they are not aware can be identified.

Value boundaries determine the extent of possible interaction with persons who possess different value systems. Rigid value systems preclude true encounters with individuals with opposing values. Similarly, rigid familiarity boundaries prevent the exploration of the unfamiliar. Individuals remain trapped in habitual patterns of living and experience a deadening of their energy, recalling the words of H.D. Thoreau: 'Multitudes of men live lives of quiet desperation'. Expressive boundaries refer to those ways in which we do or do not express ourselves. They are strongly influenced by the messages we have received as children. Applying these old childhood inhibitions to adult life can severely limit the quality of contact.

Exposure boundaries are closely associated with the uncovering of that which is hidden. Individuals do not disclose experiences which are stressful; secrecy protects the vulnerability and weakness of the person. Shlien (1984) suggests that 'much of our lifetime is geared to the production of excuses, masking images to contend with our own and each other's unwanted realities, or to create desired appearances that we wish might become realities' (p. 391). Individuals often regard exposure as shamefully discomfiting; vulnerable aspects of the self are revealed. Extending exposure boundaries involves risk, yet the result is freedom. Lynd (1958) suggests that if one can risk disclosing oneself and trust another person sufficiently to seek means of communicating what is personally shameful, the result can be in itself an experience of release, expansion and self-revelation.

This range of contact boundaries constitute the 'I' boundary. This determines what contact is permissible and possible for the individual. Within this boundary contact holds no risk for the individual. It allows individuals to contact the world around them without losing their sense of self. Outside it, contact is much more difficult since it is fraught with risk of the unknown. At the 'I' boundary, contact is uncomfortable since the consequences are less certain. Nevertheless, it is here that growth and change are possible. Contact itself, irrespective of boundaries, takes different forms.

KINDS OF CONTACT

Three different kinds of contact are described by Polster (1987): internal, interpersonal and international. Internal contact is a form of self-generated awareness: it relates to that which is experienced by us inside our skin. Enhancing good contact internally involves integrating internal contradictions, such as how to accommodate the desire to be simultaneously strong and gentle. Each element is usually engrooved in its learned mode of expression. Van de Riet, Korb and Gorrell (1988) believe that rigid polarizations exist to maintain control over the environment or oneself. They state that 'By mentally pigeonholing experience, the individual uses a two-value reference to create labels or constructs regarding life, and then proceeds to respond to the adopted labels as if those labels were, in fact, the same as the event they categorize' (p. 46). Full expression must be accorded to each polarity before accommodation can be achieved. The use of the empty chair in this regard is illustrated in Chapter 5.

Good interpersonal contact acknowledges the other person. It respects the difference between two individuals and does not seek to create sameness. 'Close identification makes good contact impossible, for only when there is a clear difference between what is you and what is not you, can you experience a meeting between the two.' (Brown, 1986; p. 80). Laura Perls (1976) points out that convention and conformity insist on sameness and agreement, 'of being one, a "we"ness without the "I" and "Thou"' (p. 224). She draws particular attention to the ignoring of the boundaries in interpersonal relationships, in marriage and in the family. The quality of interpersonal contact is diminished if either of the two parties ignores the present concerns of the other. Other instances of such diminution are cited by Polster (1987), such as relating endless trivial experiences, telling one-sided stories which do not include the listener in the interaction, and repeating the same complaints.

There are at least five components in effective interpersonal contact. Individuals need to attend to physical feelings within their bodies to contact their own experiencing; to include the consequent awareness which emerges in their interaction; to focus and receive fully the utterances of the other; to respond to the other individual; and to let the other person know that they have been heard. Focusing allows us to note not only the verbal utterances of the other but also the subtle non-verbal communications – the minute facial, postural and gestural clues that can enhance or contradict the verbal message. In responding, focusing allows us to detect when our reply does not fit. It makes possible the moment-to-moment rapport necessary for good communication. This rapport has been defined by Houston (1990) as that of 'talking across a garden gate in good weather, rather than shouting greetings from our respective house windows. We are both within our boundaries, and yet we are close enough to sometimes touch each other. We are experiencing a form of synergy, an adjusting of my breathing and other body rhythms, even my brain waves, to complement, to be nearer the experience of the other person. This rapport makes for an open learning and creative state' (p. 18).

Interpersonal contact has, in the last decade, begun to be seen in the context of a dialogical dimension in gestalt therapy. Hycner (1990) defines the dialogical as 'an approach of being open to otherness, the uniqueness of the other person, along with a desire to bring myself fully into the meeting with this other person' (p. 42). In the past, self-support was often equated with self-sufficiency. Fritz Perls' (1969b) gestalt prayer strengthened this perception. A dialogical approach stresses the relational nature of contact and, at the same time, includes the uniqueness of the two individuals concerned. According to Buber (1965), the dialogical element is not a personal attribute but only exists by virtue of the relationship. Laura Perls (1976) spoke of therapists and clients together inventing their relationship. In the dialogical approach Hycner (1990) spoke of dialogue as the ever-changing interplay of I–Thou and I–It moments. I–Thou means directness, mutuality, openness, presence, presentness. I–It is the subject–object relation: knowing, using, categorizing and analysing all the ways in which we compare one with another and I with you (Friedman, 1990). Gradually this emphasis on the dialogical is moving to the centre of gestalt therapy.

Working within such a framework, various means can be employed which help the person develop a healthy dialogical relationship. Kepner and Brien (1970) and Satir (1976) regard the five senses as central modes of contact; although Polster and Polster (1973) agree, they suggest that speech and movement are also important contact functions.

Seeing and hearing do not of themselves guarantee good contact. It is rather the quality of the sensory perception. For example, looking away or staring are two ways of diminishing contact. Polster and Polster (1973) refer to the inability to see for its own sake and make real visual contact as 'contact blindness'. Depressed persons frequently discourage contact through downcast eyes. The signal they give those who approach is 'Do not interact with me'. Increasing awareness of the kind of contact they make with the therapist is one avenue through which work on their depression may begin. The therapist can simply ask 'Are you aware of your eyes when you are talking with me?'

Seeing fully involves focusing complete attention on the person or object with which we are interacting: the attention of the good actor is centred on the other actors rather than the audience; the ham plays to the gallery. Gendlin (1978) compares focusing to talking to a person who makes a personal experience expand.

As a contact function, hearing is not of itself adequate. Individuals often admit to being 'miles away'. They are often daydreaming while others are speaking to them. They hear, but they do not listen. In listening we are attuned to the tone of voice. Tone, according to Dempsey (1961), has three main characteristics – pitch, loudness and timbre. Pitch refers to the highness or lowness of a tone, loudness relates to its strength or weakness, and timbre is the particular quality of a sound. Contact can be enhanced through the effective use of tone. A common problem is that some people listen selectively: some individuals only hear criticism while others focus on praise. This predetermined, usually unaware, selection limits ability. In couples work, the therapist can invite an individual to repeat what the other person has just said, before responding. The other person is asked to confirm its accuracy. In a group situation, the participants can be invited to pair off and to listen to each other for a few minutes without interruption. The discipline of not interrupting helps to focus the attention.

The importance of listening was attested to by Rogers (1961). He stated that 'listening is the most effective agent we know for altering the basic personality structure of the individual and improving his/her relationships and his/her communication with others'. Consequently the nature of listening needs further attention. Listening is not a passive but an active process. Attention is paramount. The listener must attend to the content of what is being said in such a manner that the speaker is aware that this is happening.

O'Leary (1986) identified three factors which can detract from the quality of listening – thinking for, thinking about, or thinking against the other person. Thinking for can take the form of interrupting the client, directing the conversation, giving advice prematurely or restating what has been said but changing its emphasis or implications. Thinking about manifests itself in the giving of 'pat' answers of the 'popular psychology' type, analysing the person's motivation or giving theoretical pronouncements of the 'everyone feels that way' type. Thinking against includes arguing or disagreeing, implying that 'you shouldn't feel that way', stating a threat to the client, or being defensive and justifying oneself.

Effective listening allows the other person to present himself/herself. The listener must think with the individual. Thinking with manifests itself in asking for more information but not directing the conversation, nodding, being actively silent, assisting individuals in examining their own feelings and finding their own answers.

Listening with is reflected in the experience of a young lady of my acquaintance who fondly recalled the attention that she received from her Aunt Joan: 'My Aunt Joan always listened to us children no matter what kind of question we had. Our experience with other older people was that we found ourselves speaking to knees or buckle belts. But whenever we talked to Aunt Joan we did not just get an answer, we got Aunt Joan. She would squat down nose-to-nose with us. We would look into her eyes. She would always repeat what we had asked to make sure she had understood it. She made us feel important. We had asked an important question, something worth bending down and listening to. Aunt Joan gave us herself and in doing so gave us self-worth'.

Touching is an obvious function with which to make good contact, yet social and cultural rules infringe on our freedom to contact one another through touch. Shaking hands is socially acceptable, although this is often so perfunctory that the nerve endings in our fingers scarcely notice the impact. The cultural prohibitions against touching results in many disguised gestures, such as patting a person's back instead of hugging him/her. The ability to touch appropriately often has to be relearnt. The gestalt group environment provides a safe context in which to experiment. Polster and Polster (1973) state that years of experience are needed before western culture can develop the grace and sensitivity that would make touching an authentic part of its existence, as it was with the Etruscans whose ancient paintings show a culture where touching was as natural as walking.

Kepner (1987) notes five important issues for therapists who use touch: therapists must use touch only to satisfy clients' perceived needs; they must also be aware of their sexuality so that they do not blur the distinction between intervention and indulgence; they must under no circumstances become sexually involved with a client – clients have the right to say 'no' to touch at any time; finally, unless there exists a strong bond and close trust between client and therapist, it is inappropriate to use touch with clients with severe pathology.

Tasting and smelling are usually viewed as minor contact functions, yet Perls, Hefferline and Goodman (1951) viewed eating as the prototype of the individual's interaction with his/her environment. Different stages in the process were outlined by Hinksman (1988): precontact is the stage of feeling hunger; this is usually followed by fore contact, where interest and energy is mobilized to prepare the food. Full contact occurs when the individual tastes the food. As the chewed food enters the digestive tract, final contact occurs. Polster and Polster (1973) point out that smell is one of the primitive contact functions which can be enhanced through the use of perfume.

Talking is a basic contact function. Most interpersonal contact involves speech. As individuals take charge of their voice they enhance the quality of their interactions. Polster and Polster (1973) point to two components of speech, voice and language. The pitch of a person's voice determines the quality of the contact made. Speaking in too low a tone requires the listener to strain to hear, and interrupts the fluidity of the process, while speaking in too high a tone can assume the quality of whining! A loud voice can overwhelm the listener. Some individuals drop their voices at the end of sentences while others maintain a monotonous unvaried tone, devoid of emotion. The value of language as a contact function is clearly illustrated by the author who can move us to varying degrees of emotion through the skilful use of words. Polster and Polster (1973) state that 'To say what one wants to say is a magnificent act of creation, easily overlooked because people talk so much' (p. 155). Language, then, is the embodiment of thought, the creation of which is man's highest achievement. Fensterheim and Baer (1976) devoted an entire book to the use of the two words 'yes' and 'no'. Methods for increasing the contact effect of language will be outlined in Chapter 4.

Contact can be diminished by what the Polsters (1973) call 'language games' (p. 156). In circumlocution, individuals talk around what they want to say. Jargon, since it has been adopted from outside the person, depersonalizes the communication. Other contact neutralizers involve the use of the phrases 'yes-but' and 'if-only', repeating oneself and over-explaining. Perls (1969b) demeans the value of verbal communication by stating that 'verbal communication is usually a lie' (p. 57). This criticism is acceptable where there is a mismatch between verbal and bodily communication: in such instances, the bodily communication must be regarded as the more reliable. Otherwise Perls' statement appears to be an overgeneralization which is unacceptable.

Physical comportment is a meaningful source of communication. Movement inhibitors block communication; expressive movement is hindered by the overall rigidity of the body. This rigidity often manifests itself in a stiff neck, where the neck is called upon to do more supporting than is necessary. Polster and Polster (1973) state that 'Flexibility is imperative to contactfulness because anything staying in sharp and unchanging focus for too long becomes dead' (p. 168). They suggest that movements that are clumsy and graceless as opposed to fluid and unimpeded indicate a compromise between an impulse and its inhibition within the person.

In gestalt therapy, expressive movement emerges as a product of the removal of inhibitions about what is happening in the here and now of the situation. Kepner (1987) points out that the use of expressive movement in a gestalt approach takes the form of experiment, (as outlined in Chapter 5), rather than exercise. He identifies five ways in which expressive movement can be developed, namely from a theme, a metaphor, microactions, body structure, and spontaneous body process.

Movement may be developed from the theme of a therapy situation as it is verbalized by the therapist or client. In a similar manner, such work may emerge from a metaphor or a figure of speech. One of the most common methods is through the naturally occurring small movements that happen during conversation. These microactions include movements of the hands and feet, and changing body posture. Some individuals take up more space than their bodies need, while others contract their bodies as much as possible. Habitual posture can serve as departure points for experiments. Spontaneous body process usually only occurs within the context of ongoing physical intervention, such as work with touch, breathing and muscular release. Gestalt therapists need to be able to deal with strong feelings before involving themselves with these methods.

The third kind of contact, namely international, depends on each side hearing the other. The building of dialogue is crucial in its development. The telling of its story by one country is pointless unless the other listens and understands what has been said. For international conflict to occur, both sides have to polarize, each viewing the other as the antithesis of its position. Unfortunately, full expression of the anger often erupts in violent behaviour, culminating in war.

THE DEVELOPMENT OF CONTACT

A prerequisite of good contact is a feeling of safety within oneself. Rosenblatt (1980) speaks of the dynamic process of support/contact. In the following example, Sam, the only black American adult in a group of whites, shares what life is like for him on a day-to-day basis. Sharing the familiar story provides the necessary support to allow Sam to come into contact with people. Polster (1987) says 'The story is an organizing agent, selecting a few events from the many which happen and giving them coherence' (p. 69).

Supporting oneself through self-disclosure

Facilitator:	'Tell us about this feeling Sam.'
Sam:	'He is a black person, a black man . . . I walk around and there are not a lot of places where I feel safe. It is hard for me to know where people are and how they are around me and what is happening. You have to go out into the world and you have to be very alert . . .'
Facilitator:	'Yes.'
Sam:	'Very tuned in to other people . . .'
Facilitator:	'To check if it is safe as a black person.'
Sam:	'Yes, Yes, Yes. I think of it as so like walking in a forest at night. All your senses are on the alert because you do not know what is happening. If you step on something, it could bite you. If you are tuned in, you are very alert to sound and movement. You know what is happening, the way people are . . . You are super-tuned in. That is one part of it. And then you know when I get home I can relax. I have made it home.'
Facilitator:	'You do not need to check any more?'
Sam:	'Right, right.'
Facilitator:	'You feel just accepted?'
Sam:	'Yes, I know that it is safe.'
Facilitator:	'How are you at home?'
Sam:	'We play, we can relax.'
Facilitator:	'Could you say I can?'
Sam:	'I can relax, I can play . . . move around, feel at ease, talk to

people, you know interact . . . I am conscious that it is very different than when I am out.'

Facilitator:	'What about now in this group?'
Sam:	'I do not know if I have played' (laughs).
Facilitator:	'Yes.'
Sam:	'But I am aware of everybody . . . I am very conscious that I am trying to extend the boundaries of where I am safe and that is what this has been about for me in terms of pushing those boundaries a little bit further . . . than I normaly work.'
Facilitator:	'A-ha.'
Sam:	'That is what this experience is right now. I can push, push, push just extend the boundaries and come into contact with other people and have a sense that it is alright. I still feel that I have to be careful.'
Facilitator:	'There is a little fear there.'
Sam:	'Yes, I am still a little careful.'
Facilitator:	'You are still experiencing your fear?'
Sam:	'Right, right, just being aware of it you know.'
Facilitator:	'Could you look at the other members in the group and check how it is to have told them how you feel? Say to yourself "I have told Jane that when I go out every day I am very aware of everyone and everything. And then when I get home I can relax, I can play, I can be myself, I can be Sam".'
Sam:	'Uh-huh. I get it, I get it.' (He rubs his hands).
Facilitator:	'What is that about Sam?'
Sam:	'Energy, strength' (laughs).

Sam pauses for a few minutes

Facilitator:	'Pay attention to that.' (A pause for a few minutes.) 'What is going on?'
Sam:	'I feel good. I am just allowing myself to relax.'
Facilitator:	'You are taking care of yourself?'
Sam:	'Yes, I need to focus to allow myself to relax.' (He stretches his body).
Facilitator:	'Where are you now?'
Sam:	'A good place.'
Facilitator:	'Maybe you do not need to do any more.'
Sam:	'Right, thank you.' Sam rubs his hands and laughs.

In this example Sam used a form of verbal support, namely self-disclosure, together with looking to increase contact. His usual pattern of involvement with the world reflected the contact/withdrawal model referred to by Smith (1986). Smith claims that individuals focus on the environment for the satisfaction of wants and withdraw into themselves for rest until dissatisfaction again arises and impels them into another cycle of contacting. Perls (1973) viewed contact and withdrawal as the 'ways we meet psychological events . . . our means of dealing at the contact boundary with objects in the field' (p. 22). He went on to say that 'If contact is prolonged it becomes ineffective or painful; if withdrawal is prolonged it interferes with the process of life. Contact and withdrawal in a rhythmic pattern are our means of satisfying our needs, of continuing the ongoing process of life itself' (p. 23).

Sam's position may be seen as one where the environment is not safe for him. Consequently he spends his time checking it out. The investment of energy in this manner prevents its flow in an outward direction; only when he returns to the safety of his home can Sam relax and interact with his surroundings. Stevens (1971) pointed out that by withdrawing from a situation, the person obtains rest and support and can then return with more energy to the problem which is creating difficulty. There are in fact two environments for Sam, one which he can handle and the other which he cannot.

Although Sam experienced difficulties, he wanted to extend his boundaries. He was able to return to the hostile environment because of the recuperation provided by the friendly environment. According to Smith (1986), a want is usually the starting point of the contact/withdrawal model, and is usually followed by a state of physiological arousal or excitement. Emotions are the expression of basic excitement, and this excitement mobilizes the muscular system into action with the environment. Smith outlines the first half of the contact episode as consisting of want–excitement–emotion. The second half consists of action–interaction–satisfaction.

Zinker (1977) embraces Smith's emphasis by describing contact in the context of a psychophysiological cycle which consists of sensation–awareness–excitement or mobilization of energy–action–contact–withdrawal. As I sit writing on this train on which I am travelling, I feel sensations in my throat and mouth. Attending to the sensation allows me to become aware of my thirst. Fortunately at this moment the trolley containing refreshments is in the carriage in which I am seated. My energy is mobilized and I order some tea. The tea bag is in the cup. Very soon if I do not do something my cup of tea will be too strong. I walk to the trolley and obtain a serviette in which to place the tea bag. This phase of judging the appropriate action to be taken has not been mentioned explicitly by Zinker, yet it constitutes an important aspect of the process, since the emergence of a new need will further delay my return to the writing. As I drink my tea the dry feeling in my throat disappears. This psychological process of engaging myself with the food is contact. Zinker states, 'The rest of my digestive system comes into focus and transforms what was originally . . . a differentiated part of the environment, into something which in this case becomes me' (p. 91). Using Zinker's terminology the drink of tea and I have become one. As I complete the satisfaction of my need, I put down the cup and return to my writing.

Gestalt therapists have devoted most attention to the part of the cycle which connects awareness and contact (Zinker, 1981). The consequence has been less consideration of the contact–withdrawal phase. Zinker states: 'We have to incorporate the notion of meditation and silences into our work. It is important to have reveries together. It is important to withdraw' (p. 17). Clarkson (1989) speaks of the culturally based tendency to hasten toward the next figure without savouring the gains made from the previous experience.

The process of withdrawal, according to Kepner (1987), involves three tasks. These are disengagement, reforming the self-boundary, and assimilation and closure. To disengage, individuals have to let go of the full contact. This may take the form of physical separation from the other. A period of quietness usually accompanies true disengagement; quietness allows the reconstitution of the self-boundary which has now been extended through the contact. The new experience is assimilated and closure is achieved.

The cycle proposed by Zinker (1977) has been extended by Clarkson (1989) to the counselling process. She points out that physical sensations such as 'a recurrent tightness in the chest, a lingering cold, an unforgiving headache or increasingly disturbed breathing' (p. 36) may lead to an awareness of the need for counselling. Mobilization of energy manifests itself in the making of an appointment with the therapist. Action takes place in the commencement of counselling. The ensuing contact allows all aspects of the problem to be identified. This leads to satisfaction as clients become more integrated in themselves, culminating in withdrawal as counselling is terminated.

OBSTACLES TO CONTACT

According to Perls, Hefferline and Goodman (1951) there are four main ways of blocking contact, namely introjection, projection, retroflection, and confluence. Polster and Polster (1973) added deflection.

Introjection

Introjection is the unquestioning acceptance of the attitudes and ideas of significant others. This thoughtless acceptance stunts personal development. Since introjectors act as they believe other people would like them to act, spontaneity becomes impossible. Corey (1985) claims that the danger of uncritical and wholesale acceptance of other people's values as one's own is that it can prevent personality integration.

The origin of introjection is in childhood. Children are born with the capacity to cope with life; however, in order to avoid conflict with significant people such as parents, or to feel accepted by them, young people uncritically accept their admonitions. As a consequence they develop judgemental attitudes towards themselves. They label themselves as 'bad', 'selfish' or 'unfair', and begin to distrust their own ability to cope. Consequently, they rely on ready-made crutches provided by these others.

A frequent introject is 'Work hard'. In this case, production is valued and the person may become work-addicted and experience difficulty in relaxing. The time-urgency of the Type A behaviour pattern as defined by Friedman and Rosenman (1974) typifies this. Time-urgent individuals wish not to waste time, for example by queuing in a bank or restaurant, since such time can be better spent on work.

Unquestioning acceptance of the generalities which constitute introjects such as 'Never trust anybody' and 'Men do not cry', condemn many people to lonely lives. Introjectors wish life to remain as it is, since any change would challenge their second-hand value system. They seek to control their environment by adherence to rules and regulations which have not been assimilated. To do otherwise would result in anxiety and defensiveness.

Some teachers promote introjection by encouraging students to memorize pages without comprehension, simply to pass an examination. Since this activity achieves results in the short term, the introjectors persuade themselves that the 'foreign body' is good in itself. They may continue the activity long after it has achieved the desired result.

Introjectors try to please others. They find it difficult to distinguish between what they really feel and what others want them to feel. The environment impinges on them to such an extent that the contact boundary is pushed so far inside themselves that there is nearly nothing left of the 'self'. This creates two problems for individuals: firstly, developing their own personality is difficult, since they focus on the codes of other people for living, and secondly, the introjection of contradictory concepts creates continuous internal conflicts. (Perls, 1973).

Introjection comes into operation when individuals fail to recognize thoughts and attitudes as not belonging to themselves. They view them as their own and resist their dislodgement as if they were part of themselves. Energy is invested in the preservation of previously acquired injunctions, rather than in their destruction. According to Zinker (1977), 'The person who blocks between awareness and energy mobilization suffers from introjection; he/she has swallowed other people's ideas about what is right and wrong and is unable to locate his/her own energy'.

Perls, Hefferline and Goodman (1951) distinguish between introjection and assimilation. That which is assimilated is not taken in as a whole; it is first destroyed completely and then transformed and absorbed selectively, according to the needs of the organism. An introject, on the other hand, consists of a way of acting, feeling and evaluating which individuals take into their system of behaviour, but which they have not assimilated in such a way as to make it a genuine part of themselves. Polster and Polster (1973) found that introjectors invest energy into passively incorporating what the environment provides. Problems arise, however, when the world does not behave consistently with their established patterns. They must then devote their energy to accepting things as they are.

Projection

Projection allows individuals to hive off unwanted attributes on to others, and make these others responsible for feelings and attitudes that are essentially part of their own make-up. In this process, individuals do not accept their own feelings but transfer them to others. Such clients will accuse people of rejecting them, while being unaware and unaccepting of the fact that it is they themselves who are rejecting others.

Projectors usually blame other people. Typical projection statements are: 'Nobody cares about me', 'It is all my mother's fault, she never loved me as a child', and 'I never had a chance'. The blamer is usually a lonely person since few people will listen sympathetically. Individuals project those aspects of behaviour which conflict with their introjects: this allows them to assume the role of victim as opposed to aggressor; they do not realize that they are the instigators of the behaviour. Paranoia is an extreme form of projection, where paranoid individuals make the environment responsible for what originates in themselves.

In projection, clients interrupt the adequate expression of personal experience which is usually aggressive in nature. The 'I' is excluded from the feeling and so the sense of responsibility is diminished. Since clients interrupt their own process, the intensity of the force experienced from outside can be quite strong. The interesting aspect of projection is that the person(s) on to whom the feeling is projected, usually possess(es) the characteristic. This allows a camouflage of the true situation. The perceived boundary between themselves and the other is blurred.

Retroflection

Retroflection means 'to turn sharply back against'. The desire to act in a particular way, e.g. to hug another, is blocked and converted into personal muscular tension. Retroflectors do to themselves what they wish to do to others, or others to do to them. For example, they may desire to punish others but when they encounter resistance they are angry with themselves instead. These retroflections express themselves as manipulations of the body, such as tensing the arms and shoulders and clenching the teeth when repressing anger.

Retroflectors split their personality into 'doer' and 'done to'. Originally they tried to satisfy their needs by interacting with the environment; however, the surroundings were inimicable to their efforts and they withdrew into themselves. Fear of further rebuff prevented them interacting with the environment.

Retroflectors hold equal and opposing tension in their muscular system, since their energy is divided and competes against itself. Angry retroflectors wish to express their anger, but fear of retaliation causes them to hold it back. Retroflectors often speak of 'myself', such as 'I am ashamed of myself' and 'I am afraid of myself'. Perls (1969b) lists narcissism and suicide as extreme forms of retroflection. Since retroflectors fear complete rejection by the environment they engage in retroflection, which gives at least partial satisfaction.

Narcissists are surer of their self-admiration than of being valued by others. Zinker (1977) states, 'When the murderously angry person overdoes his/her retroflecting, he/she kills himself' (p. 103).

Confluence

Confluent individuals experience no boundary between themselves and their environment. They cannot tolerate difference, with the result that they will frequently give in to other people or try to change them to make them more similar to themselves. Confluent individuals usually use the pronoun 'we' rather than 'I'. They lose all sense of their own identity and their own needs; the boundary between themselves and the environment is not experienced. True interpersonal contact is not possible since the other is not viewed as separate. On the other hand, withdrawal from the other does not occur. Harman (1982) says, 'Confluent people see to it that nothing new happens; yet at the same time little that is interesting or exciting happens in their relationship' (p. 47).

A confluent relationship between two individuals requires that they agree not to disagree. If a difference emerges, the person who has created the change situation may, according to Polster and Polster (1973), feel obliged to apologize or to make restitution for breach of contract. Hinksman (1988) speaks of the apparent nature of confluence in a person with a hysterical personality pattern in the group situation. These individuals have many things they want to share in the group, but they do not know where to start, or may engage in random spontaneity or compulsive behaviour. The experience for them is, he states, 'like walking in fog, or hearing particles of speech, or having glimpses of images or just feeling blank' (p. 71).

Deflection

Deflection seeks to interrupt or turn aside from contact with another person. The language games outlined earlier are means of deflecting contact. Deflection is experienced through a fleeting sense of the environment, and may be characterized by avoidance of eye-contact, politeness, excessive use of language, and the lessening of emotional expression. The interference with contact may occur by either the receiver or the sender of the message. 'Senders' states Harman (1982) 'put out their messages with a 'scatter-gun' effect: sometimes they hit the target if they aim in the right direction, while at other times their message may miss its target entirely. Receivers deflect contact with armoured consistency, so that few messages have impact on them' (p. 46). Senders are usually at a loss as to why they do not get what they need, while receivers are unaffected by the interaction. Deflectors move from topic to topic without dwelling at length on any one area.

The use of these mechanisms is not always unhealthy: the chief difference between healthy and unhealthy uses is that in the former the person acts with awareness. Thus, employees may withhold their anger against the boss if they realize that such behaviour may have undesirable consequences.

OBSTACLES TO INTERPERSONAL CONTACT IN A GROUP SITUATION

Frew (1986) relates each of the five mechanisms for avoiding contact to three phases of group development, namely, orientation, conflict, and cohesion. In the orientation phase, members are concerned with their own safety and endeavour to locate themselves in the environment as quickly as possible. Introjectors rely upon the leader to provide structure to the experience. Projective individuals attribute to the leader or other group members characteristics that are not really there. Retroflectors speak little, while confluent persons tend to emphasize the similarities among group participants rather than the differences. Deflectors divert eye-contact, or speak in short sentences. Harman (1982) states that deflection and projection are particularly pervasive in the early stages of a group.

In the conflict phase, members assert control over the direction of the group and deal with power and authority issues. Introjectors shift their attention to informal leaders who begin to emerge in the group. Projective individuals disown their own control needs by perceiving other members as taking over the group. Retroflectors modify their feelings with regard to the direction of the group, and keep some of the emotion within themselves. Confluent individuals minimalize differences between themselves and other subgroup members. Deflective persons address feeling comments relating to the group process to participants in general, rather than to the member for whom it is intended. Other manifestations of deflection may include using humour or story-telling, or suggesting a break to obviate the emerging conflict within the group. Harman (1982) points out that the responses of deflectors will often seem inappropriate or out of context, and they may seem confused and off the mark.

Cohesion is marked by a high level of participation and emotional comfort. Introjectors may accept statements by the group leader concerning the termination of the group, without attending to their feelings concerning it. Projective individuals may re-own material which has been disowned onto the group leader or other participants. Retroflectors may restrain themselves from sharing positive and negative feelings, and leave the group with unfinished business. Healthy confluence, according to Latner (1982), is the experience of bonding, of being loved and loving. There is a sense of being part of the whole in this final stage. Clarkson (1989) states that 'Learning to appreciate . . . our experiences at points of completion seems to be one of the most significant and profound moments of existence' (p. 123). A prolongation of this feeling, however, can indicate unhealthy confluence and an attempt to resist closure. Deflectors seek to ameliorate their sense of impending loss by planning a reunion, or referring to future possible meetings between different group members.

Chapter 4

Awareness techniques: language and non-verbal communication

INTRODUCTION

A discussion of gestalt therapy must include some reference to technique. However, learning the mechanics is not what gestalt therapy is about: trainee gestalt therapists should not be introduced immediately to the use of skills. Much time must first be spent working on their own personal growth issues, where they experience directly the use of techniques in the context of their own difficulties. In this way they will come to understand that counselling procedures are not meant to be used in the manipulation of clients, but rather in their service.

Polster and Polster (1973) recommend that therapists use their own experience as an essential ingredient in the therapy process, remembering that they are more than mere responders or givers of feedback, or catalysts that do not change themselves. The personality of the therapist influences the quality of the interaction with the client. In this regard, Moustakas (1974) advocated that therapists should allow their talents and skills, their total experience as human beings, to blend naturally into the relationship. This view is supported by Page (1984): 'The techniques of gestalt therapy are used in conjunction with the therapist's own style of expression in the therapeutic situation. There is no 'right' way to employ them' (p. 192).

Gestalt therapy possesses a wide variety of techniques that are used to strengthen what individuals feel in the present. They emerge in the process of therapy and are tailored to the particular situation. Therapists demonstrate their skill by this matching of a particular technique to the situation presented. The goal of gestalt therapy, namely the self-empowerment of the client, must not be lost in the forest of technique. In this chapter it is not intended to present a recipe for technical success; rather, it is hoped that the knowledge base of the reader may be expanded by illustrating techniques with an appropriate example, or a transcript of an actual session.

An attempt has been made in recent years to consider the use of techniques in a more rigorous fashion, as outlined in Chapter 7. However, the quality of their effect can be evaluated only if the technique has been used appropriately in the first place. It is sometimes claimed (cf. Corey, 1985) that some therapists who are attracted to gestalt procedures are more influenced by their dramatic impact than their potential for therapeutic change. Corey states: 'Some therapists have become so enthralled with Perls' dynamic personality and style that they mimic only his style, without fully understanding and incorporating the conceptual framework of gestalt therapy' (p. 305).

There is an accepted frame of gestalt technique as illustrated by Corey (1985), Dryden (1984), and Patterson (1973). All of these authors describe language exercises, such as changing questions to statements, use of the personal pronoun 'I', empty-chair work to encourage dialogue, dream-work and reversal experiments. In the next section we consider language approaches.

AWARENESS TECHNIQUES: LANGUAGE

In gestalt therapy it is not sufficient to pay attention only to *what* clients say: the precise manner in which they express themselves can be as significant as the content. The following are aspects of language use which gestalt therapists note:

- Making 'I' statements;
- Omitting qualifiers and disclaimers;
- Using the active voice;
- Changing verbs;
- Changing questions to statements;
- Being specific;
- Making demands;
- Changing the form of questions;
- Being present-centred.

Making 'I' statements

Through the use of 'I' language, the therapist endeavours to assist clients to be accountable for their behaviour, thoughts and feelings. Responsible clients do not blame outside forces, such as other people, or situational factors, for their own deficiencies. Thus clients are invited to replace impersonal language such as 'one', 'they' and 'we', with 'I' statements which allow them to acknowledge responsibility for themselves. Within a group, clients are not permitted to speak for anyone but themselves. Sentences such as 'they made me do that', or 'she did not wake me', attribute blame to others. Therapists seek to evoke in clients an awareness of their defensiveness, by inviting them to repeat the sentence and to replace the impersonal term with 'I'. This results in direct subjective statements. At the beginning clients may experience a feeling of strangeness in the use of 'I', proportionate to the extent that they have displaced their own process onto others through generalizations.

Example 1: making 'I' statements

Therapist:	'Tell me a little about your husband.'
Client:	'You feel awful the minute you see him coming in from work and then you wonder what you will say to him.'
Therapist:	'Could you say "I feel awful the minute I see him coming in from work"?'
Client:	'Oh but I do'.
Therapist:	'Yes, I know that, but I want you to experience it more fully by putting it in the first person singular.'
Client:	'Alright. I feel terrible the minute I see Martin coming in from work. I do not know what to say to him.'

Using the impersonal pronoun 'you' enabled Mary to distance herself from her feelings. The change to 'I' altered the impersonal to personal. Other examples of impersonal terms include 'everyone', 'anyone', 'most people', 'some people'.

Omitting qualifiers and disclaimers

Qualifiers and disclaimers allow people to avoid committing themselves to feelings, thoughts or actions. Some of the most frequently used disclaimers are 'maybe', 'perhaps', 'I suppose', 'kind of', 'sort of', 'possibly', 'I guess', 'probably', 'a bit'.

Example 2: omitting qualifiers

Client:	'I was kind of disappointed that Clare did not visit me.'
Therapist:	'You were disappointed.'
Client:	'Yes I was disappointed. I might talk to Clare about it.'
Therapist:	'You might.'
Client:	'I will talk to Clare about it.'

By using the qualifier 'kind of', the client avoided experiencing the fullness of the disappointment; use of the word 'might' indicated a certain reluctance to share this disappointment with Clare. In both instances, the client lessened the impact of the message. By repeating the language used, the therapist increased awareness of how disclaimers diminish communication. Alternatively, clients can be invited directly to omit qualifiers. In so doing, ambivalent messages are changed into clear and direct statements. A frequently used disclaimer is the word 'but'.

Example 3: 'but' into 'and'

Client:	'I care about John but it makes me angry when he never expresses what he feels.'
Therapist:	'Could you say "I care about John *and* it makes me angry when he never expresses what he feels".'
Client:	'I care about John and it makes me angry when he does not express his feelings.'

Use of the word 'but' in this way discounted the immediately preceding statement – it implied that the second part was the more important, and in this manner the significant feeling of care was ignored. By inviting the client to replace 'but' by 'and', each part of what was said was accepted and given equal emphasis. The second part did not negate the first.

Using the active voice

Using the passive voice allows clients to avoid responsibility for their behaviour. Passons (1975) states that individuals may speak that way because they feel controlled and manipulated. The following example illustrates this.

Example 4: changing the passive to the active voice

Client:	'When Tommy's brothers and their wives come to visit us I am just pushed outside the circle. They talk about people I do not know and places I have never visited. I am excluded completely.'
Therapist:	'Could you say "I exclude myself"?'
Client:	'I do not. I am sitting there, but I am not included in the conversation.'
Therapist:	'I know that that is how you feel but could you try saying "I exclude myself" and see how it feels.'
Client:	'I . . . exclude myself . . . I do . . . I suppose I do really . . . . I do keep myself apart from the conversation.'

As a result of the counsellor's suggestion to experiment with a sentence which used the active voice, the client became aware of how he/she was maintaining a helpless position.

Changing verbs

Particular verbs can permit clients to believe that certain actions are outside their control. They are encouraged to become aware of their resistance to change by their use of such verbs as 'can't', 'ought', 'have to', and 'need'. In altering these, their reluctance to do certain things becomes apparent. Clients are faced with the knowledge that they do have choices in their lives.

Example 5: 'can't' into 'won't'

Client:	'I can't forgive Mary for not inviting me to her wedding.'
Therapist:	'Try saying, "I *won't* forgive Mary for not inviting me to her wedding".'
Client:	'I won't forgive Mary for not inviting me to her wedding.' (Silence). 'That is true. I just won't forgive her.'

By changing 'can't' to 'won't', clients realize that they have control over the situation. Other alternatives are 'I am not willing', or 'I choose not to . . .'. In the above example, the client recognizes that he/she will not forgive Mary. This is a necessary step in the process of discovering what the underlying feelings might be in not forgiving. Only if the fact is first acknowledged can feelings be identified, discussed and worked through.

Use of the word 'can't' or 'cannot' usually signifies that individuals are unwilling to change their present behaviour. However, not every 'can't' can be changed into 'won't'. In general, using 'won't' for 'can't' assists individuals to own and accept their power by taking responsibility for their decisions (Corey, 1985). They are no longer able to blame other people or outside events.

'Ought', 'should', 'have to', and 'supposed to'

The words 'ought', 'should', 'have to', and 'supposed to' signify that the person has introjected advice or standards of behaviour from other people. Introjectors have never decided what they want for themselves – they are amenable to control. Their actions are usually determined by what others think that they 'ought to' or 'should' do. Within institutions and organizations such as armies, the police force and religious orders, the model follower can be an introjector of the institute's or organization's rules and regulations. This is not to say that all model followers are introjectors. Indeed, many model persons in these organizations have internalized and assimilated the values and regulations as their own. 'Ought' and 'should' frequently impose limitations and have nothing to do with real moral obligation. The therapist increases clients' awareness by inviting clients to replace 'should' by 'choose to'.

Example 6: 'have' into 'choose'

Client:	'I have to spend my summer holidays with my parents.
Therapist:	'Who says?'
Therapist:	'Well nobody, I just know I should.'

Therapist:	'You should.'
Client:	'Well my parents would be disappointed if I did not.'
Therapist:	'What about saying "I choose to spend my summer holidays with my parents"?'
Client:	'Mm – well' (Reflects). 'I choose to spend one week with my parents. I want to spend the second week with my friends.'

By changing 'have to' to 'choose to', clients are enabled to differentiate between what they choose to do and what they want to do. Use of 'choose to' highlights the choices which they can make. They can then be responsible for their actions, feelings and behaviours. This sense of responsibility is essential for personal growth and development. The use of 'should', 'ought', 'have to' and 'supposed to', on the other hand, usually leads to a feeling of helplessness.

'Need' and 'want'

People often use the word 'need' when in fact the appropriate word is 'want'. Using the word 'need' gives a situation a feeling of urgency which often may not be warranted. What we 'need' psychologically is often debated among psychologists. Glasser (1984) states that there are four psychological needs – power, love, fun and freedom. Maslow (1956) conceptualized the situation somewhat differently. He spoke of physiological, security and belonging needs, the need for love, self-esteem and self-actualization. There are many situations which are preferences rather than psychological needs. To be loved may be seen as a need, whereas to be loved by Bill is a matter of preference. Some needs are global and the specific fulfilment of them can take many forms.

Example 7: 'can't' into 'choose not'

Client:	'I am heartbroken. I can't live without Mary. I need her.'
Therapist:	'You can't live without Mary.'
Client:	'No. I can't.'
Therapist:	'Try saying "I choose not to live without Mary".'
Client:	'Well it is very difficult.'
Therapist:	'It is very difficult but you can live.'
Client:	'Yes I can even though it is difficult. I want her to stay.'

By using 'choose not' rather than 'can't', the client realized that he could live without Mary. What he perceived as a need is now viewed as a want, and loses its melodramatic nature.

Changing questions into statements

In gestalt therapy, the therapist recognizes that questions are often judgemental hooks: clients manipulate the therapist into extricating them from the difficulties they are experiencing. Statements are a more effective and authentic mode of communication. They normally concern thoughts, feelings or actions of clients in the here-and-now of their awareness and responsibility.

Example 8: changing questions into statements

Client: 'Why am I feeling like this?'
Therapist: 'What is your guess?'
Client: 'Well I guess I have always felt insecure since I was left on my own in the dark as a child.'

Rather than interpreting or supplying an answer, the therapist invited the client to explore his/her own internal frame of reference to discover what was the underlying issue.

Being concrete/being specific

Difficulty in communication often arises when people globalize and intellectualize. The therapist invites clients to move from these generalizations to specific instances.

Example 9: being specific

Client: 'My stepmother was always comparing me with other children of my own age and criticizing me.
Therapist: 'With whom did she compare you?'
Client: 'Lots of kids around us.'
Therapist: 'Can you remember any of their names?'
Client: 'Well one girl, Angela, was very good at school and my mother always wanted me to be as good as she was at English.'

Concreteness can be of particular value when a client presents several topics. The therapist can ask 'On which of these concerns do you wish to work?' The client is thus enabled to focus on a specific issue and at the same time remain self-directing.

Making demands

Closely related to concreteness is the ability of the client to make demands on others.

Example 10: making demands

Client: 'I would like Stephen to be home by 6.30 so that I could go out and do the shopping before the store closes.'
Therapist: 'Could you say that directly to him?'
             (the therapist places an empty chair in front of the client.)

~nt:	'Stephen, I would like you to be in by 6.30 so that I can go shopping.'
Therapist:	'You would like or you want?'
Client:	'Oh . . . I want him in by that time.'
Therapist:	'Could you tell him that?'
Client:	'Stephen, I want you to be home by 6.30 on Friday because I want to go shopping.'

By making a demand in this manner, the client makes it clear to Stephen that he/she wants him to be home at 6.30.

Changing the form of questions

Gestalt therapists carefully choose the form of the questions they use. 'Why' questions are avoided at all times, as they encourage rationalizations and intellectualizations. 'How' and 'what' questions, on the other hand, enable individuals to structure their experience and mobilize self-support.

Example 11: 'what' and 'how' rather than 'why' questions

Client:	'Well I guess I have always felt insecure since I was sexually abused.'
Therapist:	'How do you feel insecure.'
Client:	'I never get good grades in school.'
Therapist:	'What grades to you get.'

'Why' questions analyse motivation and encourage clients to be abstract rather than concrete. 'What' and 'How' questions are more likely to bring the feelings associated with an experience into awareness. They increase awareness of sensations, behaviour, feelings and experiences.

- Sensations: What are you aware of in your body right now?
- Behaviour: What are you doing?
- Feeling: How are you feeling?
- Experience: How do you feel when you remember that George said that he loved you?

Example 12: using 'how' instead of 'why'

Client:	'My mother said that she missed me.'
Therapist:	'How did you feel when your mother said that?'

Being present-centred

Being present-centred involves asking clients to attend to what they are presently experiencing. Rosenblatt (1975) refers to this as the principle of immediacy. He believed that what the client discloses in therapy is not experienced as part of a distant past but as a living present, a current unfinished situation. Perls (1969b, p. 79) placed considerable emphasis on the immediate moment: he said 'My function as a therapist is to help you to the here and now and to frustrate you in any attempt to break out of this'. Questions such as 'What are you doing now?' enable clients to enter their present experiencing, rather than engaging in story-telling of past events. Even descriptions of past situations can be present-centred by inviting clients to tell their story in the present tense. This allows them to re-experience the feelings associated with the events. Perls (1976) states that 'if a patient is finally to close the book on his past problems, he must close it in the present'. If past problems have been dealt with adequately, they will no longer intrude in the individual's everyday life.

Rosenblatt (1976) points out that all we can be really sure of is now. He states 'What is passed, past, is already changed, perhaps forgotten, certainly altered by memory. And what is to come in the future is uncertain, unreal, only a possibility'. Involvement in the present precludes the development of anxiety since energy is directed to the present activity. Perls (1969b) states: 'If you are in the now you are creative, you are inventive. If you have your senses ready, if you have your eyes and ears open, you find a solution'. Through awareness of the present, unfinished situations surface and achieve closure.

Example 13: being present-centred

Client:	'I was 6 years old when my mother started to hit me with a leather strap.'
Therapist:	'Could you say "I am 6 years old and my mother is hitting me with a leather strap", and then continue the story as if it were happening now.'

Present-centredness involves being aware of sensations, breathing, gestures and voice. Clients focus on such aspects as holding their breath, clenching their fists, speaking in a shrill tone and interrupting contact with the therapist by looking away. Being present-centred includes paying attention not only to the use of language, but to body messages as well. These will be considered in the next section.

AWARENESS TECHNIQUES: NON-VERBAL COMMUNICATION

Becoming aware of the body

The importance of the body in gestalt therapy is paramount. Perls (1969b, p. 57) describes how the therapist attends to the process of psychosomatic language. 'Don't listen to the words' he said 'just listen to what the voice tells you, what the posture tells you, what the image tells you . . . the facial expression, the psychosomatic language. If you use your eyes and ears, then you see that everyone expresses himself in one way or another'.

Awareness of the body is facilitated in the following ways:

1. Eliciting body sensations from the client;
2. Naming the feeling;
3. Giving feedback to the client;
4. Mirroring body language;
5. Undoing retroflections.

Eliciting body sensations from the client

In the following example the client, Sarah, was discussing how she compared herself unfavourably to other people, and how this affected the way that she felt about herself.

Example 14: eliciting body sensations

Sarah:	'These feelings do not last but there is a residue there.'
Therapist:	'Residue?'
Sarah:	'Yes, a leftover kind of feeling.'
Therapist:	'Can you locate that feeling in your body?'
Sarah:	'I suppose in my chest.'
Therapist:	'In your chest?'
Sarah:	'Yes, I have this feeling in my chest.'

In a group setting, participants can be invited to close their eyes in order to block out external stimuli. They can then be asked to become aware of areas of tension in their bodies. In this manner, they may become sensitive to a lump in their throat, clenched hands, or a cramp in their stomach. Alternatively, the therapist can guide bodily experience by directing the attention of group members to different parts of their body in turn.

Example 15: exploring body awareness in groups

Facilitator:	'Now you can close your eyes. As you do so become aware that you are blocking out all external stimuli in order to pay attention to your body. Now focus on your feet, let your feet become the centre of your awareness. Check each part of your foot – your toes – the toes on your right foot – your right ankle – your right calf – the toes on your left foot.' (Continuing in this manner the therapist increases clients' awareness of each part of their body in turn.)

Central to body awareness is the manner in which individuals breathe. Perls, Hefferline and Goodman (1951) gave special attention to this. Participants are helped to relax when they focus on their breathing.

Example 16: paying attention to breathing

'Close your eyes. Become aware of your body. Now turn attention to your breathing. How do you take breath into your body and leave it out again? As you pay attention to your breathing notice how it becomes deeper. Are there any blocks to your breathing? If so, where are they? Notice in detail the whole process of breathing, how you breathe – in through your nose, down through your throat, chest, into your belly and how you exhale from your belly to your chest up through your throat and out through your mouth.'

Name the feeling

Once a feeling is located within the body, awareness is increased by inviting the individual to give it an outline and to identify its size, colour and/or texture. When this has been done, the client gives the feeling a voice. In example 14, Sarah had identified a feeling in her chest.

Example 17: naming the feeling

Therapist:	'How does this feeling feel?'
Sarah:	'Well, heavy.'
Therapist:	'Could you outline it for me?'
Sarah:	'Well it goes up on the left and across to the centre and comes back down this way in the shape of a triangle' (Sarah uses her hand to delineate this triangular shape).
Therapist:	'So it is a heavy feeling that is this big.' (Therapist designates the area to allow the client to obtain a better sense of it). 'Could you give the feeling a voice?'
Sarah:	'I am the feeling in Sarah's chest. I have been here for a long time. I am here anytime Sarah is compared unfavourably to other people.'

Giving feedback to the client

Perls, Hefferline and Goodman (1951) felt that almost all individuals have lost the sense of large areas of their body. For clients, body awareness is often difficult and anxiety-provoking at first. As already stated in Chapter 1, Perls' attention to the body was based on the character-armour theory of Wilhelm Reich (1969). Reich believed that resistances became located in muscular tensions. Through feeling the body, Reich could assess the muscular armouring and locate the focal point of bound anxiety. Muscular tension, he believed, was self-produced. Gestalt therapists are aware of this and when they notice non-verbal behaviour in clients, they share their observations with them.

Example 18: giving feedback to the client

Therapist: 'When you talk about your father, I notice that you clench your teeth. Are you aware of that?'

Mirroring body language

An alternative method of increasing clients' awareness of their body language is for the therapist to mirror it to them.

Example 19: mirroring the body language of clients

Client: 'My mother did not love me' (hand over mouth).
Therapist: (Puts own hand over mouth and leaves it there.)
Client: 'Well, I feel as if I am betraying my mother by admitting that she did not love me.'

These two aspects of gestalt therapy – becoming aware of language and of the body – provide the foundation and set the scene for more sophisticated techniques such as experiments. These will be discussed in Chapter 5.

Chapter 5

Experiments

INTRODUCTION

Experiments, or enactments as they are sometimes called, are based upon the principle that learning requires action. Zinker (1977) says of an experiment: 'It transforms talking about into doing, stale reminiscing and theorizing into being fully here with all one's imagination, energy and excitement' (p.123). Experiments are ways in which people make discoveries about themselves by attempting new activities. They are novel in character and deliberate in nature. In the safety of a gestalt group, people engage in behaviours which in a less secure setting they might be fearful to employ. The process itself, even if not completed, can be enriching. For example, while involved in an experiment a person may stop abruptly. Rather than offering platitudes, the therapist or group should allow the individual to stay with the interruption since it is thus that blocks to appropriate action are often discovered.

Experiments may be used in order to focus on individuals' awareness of how they behaved in a previous situation. For example, Mary, who has to accompany her husband to social events relating to his job, becomes frozen when it is necessary for her to circulate. Within gestalt therapy, Mary can re-enact this situation with other group members and come to an understanding of the factors which block her. The previously resisted action becomes a possibility within the group. Moreno's (1946) influence on gestalt therapy can be seen in experiments. Through his use of psychodrama he emphasized that a person is more likely to make discoveries by participating in an event rather than by merely talking about it. This approach acknowledged the force of direct experience and moved therapy beyond reliance on the interpretive function so central to the psychoanalytic ethos.

FOUR STAGES OF AN EXPERIMENT

Zinker (1977) states that an elegant experiment, or more accurately, a series of experiments, is like a symphony. There is a beginning movement in which information is introduced and a general theme emerges. In the following passage, Raymond is talking about tensions in his body. He thinks that he is relaxed when in fact he is just not acknowledging what is there.

Stage One: identification of general theme

Raymond: 'Ah . . . it goes back to my wanting to be somehow in control of myself . . . just as I say it now I am aware that that is not the way to do it. If I feel in touch with myself, I feel more in control of myself. I suppose it is a heady thing really to ignore what is going on around and to get a notion then that I am okay.'

Therapist: 'So you feel that by ignoring these signals from your body that you are in control?'

Raymond: 'Yes but it is forced on me now that that is not the way it is . . . that my thoughts are not definitely in line with activity . . . my feeling that I was relaxed and the physical evidence I can see in my hands. My hand was not letting loose and I was saying I was relaxed when in fact I was not.'

The general theme has emerged, namely, how Raymond feels in control when he is using his head and ignoring what is going on in his body. The session now moves into the second stage, where many details are filled in and the person's understanding of the theme is enriched.

Stage Two: enrichment of understanding of theme

Therapist: 'And where has that pattern come from?'

Raymond: 'It goes back a bit and it relates to what is coming up for me . . . sometimes my face is impassive and non-expressive. Years ago I learnt to be impassive. My entire self learnt to be impassive, to try to keep control of the situation at home. My father was a very heavy drinker; he would come in in the evenings and I can picture him very clearly even to this day. He would come in and my mother would get mad at him for drinking and being drunk. He was quite messy when he was drunk and she would start arguing and this went on for years. We as children were fed up with it and frustrated by it. I used to say to my mother "Forget the arguments just say nothing and pretend it does not affect you" and that is what I was doing . . . feelings of sorrow . . . feelings of shame as well, I was feeling ashamed of him. I was feeling sorry for my mother for what she had to go through and I can feel the tension of the situation and trying to deal with that and the way I did it was, in retrospect now, to remain still and make it go away. I did not do anything to provoke anything . . . it was pointless showing that emotion or arguing when it did not make any difference to him. He would still come in drunk at another time and upset us all over again. I learnt that very easily, very quickly too . . . and that is what I used, that is my way of dealing with that.'

The third movement now begins to emerge, where the session uncovers an important developmental dynamic of the larger theme, namely, looking cold and distant as a way of being in control, which had become part of how he behaved in general.

Stage Three: uncovering the developmental dynamic

Therapist: 'So if you denied to yourself these emotions existed you did not have to suffer pain?'

Raymond: 'I was aware they existed but I put things at bay – and that has been a pattern for me (pauses). The "front" was necessary because I did not want to be arguing about it. I felt that being quiet and being stiff and poker-faced was a way of not provoking any further reaction. It was scary as well. I suppose it was my way as a young person of dealing with it . . . but I think a lot of people said that I can have that effect on people sometimes . . . looking very cold and distant or my face is unmoving or not very expressive.'

The third movement usually moves into the heart of the experiment. In this instance, the empty chair becomes a person from the past, with whom the client has unfinished business.

Therapist: 'Casting your mind back, what age were you when you remember being quiet, stiff, poker-faced and scared?'

Raymond: 'Somewhere between seven and ten – around eight, I think.'

Therapist: 'What does it feel like to be that eight-year-old?'

Raymond: 'It feels helpless and powerless.'

Therapist: 'Would you like to tell your mother or your father about these feelings?

Raymond: 'Sure.'

Therapist: 'Well let us get a chair. Here we are. Now to whom do you want to express your feelings, your mother or your father?'

Raymond: 'Ah . . . I suppose both really, in the sense that I would have something to say to both of them – different things to

	say to each person. But I think my father more so . . . I would not have spoken to my father about that . . . So I would rather speak to him.'
Therapist:	'So your father is sitting in this chair and you are that powerless child and instead of being impassive you are now going to speak your emotions. What comes up for you?'
Raymond:	'I am a bit scared sitting so close to you . . . that is the first thing because I do not normally talk to you . . . I very rarely talk to you . . . You never sit down and listen to me, to what I have to say. It strikes me you are interested in your own thing and you do not have an awful lot of time for me anyway. I can see you now again, as I am speaking to you now that you are drunk . . . that is how I remember you . . . I feel the same things I always feel – very tense about what is going to happen, about what you are going to do . . . the way you talk, the way you slur your speech, the way you act the idiot and make us upset. I am upset for Mary and Paul and Mother, most of all, I suppose because she had to put up with you all the time and I want you to know that.'
Therapist:	'What are your hands saying now Raymond?'
Raymond:	'They are telling me that as usual I am very tense about it and nervous and apprehensive – not that he knows. You do not know that because you do not really care in the first place . . . I do not feel it anyway . . . I mean you are grand when you are sober . . . the next day it is all a thing of the past. You could be talking away and laughing but I will not make conversation next day. I just will not do that just because it is all gone for you. You expect me then to act as if nothing had happened and you want us all to be one big happy family again. I do not want to do that because it hurts me too much and it hurts all of us too much and I cannot forget it the next day and I want you to know that as well.'
Therapist:	'It hurts you too much.'
Raymond:	'Yes . . . (begins to cry) . . . 'How could you . . .'
Therapist:	(Notices clenched jaw, choking sobs). 'What about letting your jaw drop and letting out the sound?'
Raymond:	(Sobs for several minutes.)

The fourth stage is now reached as the client moves towards a sense of resolution and integration.

Stage Four: resolution and integration

Therapist: 'What is going on for you now Raymond?'

Raymond: 'I feel an awful lot inside of me. I am just in touch with myself, which is something I would not have been before as well as being in touch with him.'

Therapist: 'How does it feel to be that way with your father?'

Raymond: 'Hurt and soft and vulnerable.'

Therapist: 'How does it feel to be hurt and soft and vulnerable with your father?'

Raymond: 'Fine'. (To father) 'I want you to see how you really hurt me' (Pause). (To therapist). 'It is fine to say what I feel. That way he does not control me. The other way he did.'

Therapist: 'So your father controlled you?'

Raymond: 'Yes when he got drunk I did not allow myself to show any feeling about it and this became a pattern in my communication with others. By not showing feeling I felt that they could not hurt me.'

Therapist: 'And now?'

Raymond: 'Now I realize how phoney that is – it is like being a mask.'

Therapist: 'Raymond, would you like to sit there?' (pointing to empty chair for a minute).

Raymond: 'I have reservations about sitting in my father's seat.'

Therapist: 'What is that about?'

Raymond: 'That is about me feeling as I do now – an awful lot inside of me. I am not in touch with what he is feeling right now. I am just in touch with myself which is something I would not have been before. I can see how I put up that shield.'

Therapist: 'How does it feel to have other people in the group see you cry?'

Raymond: 'Fine.'

Therapist: 'Could you check that out?'

Raymond: (Looks around the group). 'Yes, it is fine.'

An experiment always grows out of the life of the client. Therapists must stay finely attuned to the client in order to discover those moments in which the groundwork for an experiment is laid. In the above example, the theme emerges when Raymond identifies being in control as ignoring what is going on in his body. At this moment the therapist knows that Raymond needs to express fully what has been left unsaid. However, therapists must be patient and acquire the history of a particular behaviour, otherwise they do not set a relevant scene for the experiment.

The empty chair allows Raymond to express his unresolved feelings towards his father. He contacts his father's drunken behaviour and the emotions he had swallowed. The power he gave away by remaining silent in the past is reclaimed in the present. Telling stories only about his father's drunkenness would have been 'aboutism'. Polster and Polster (1973) state that the experiment in gestalt therapy is an attempt to counter the 'aboutism' deadlock by bringing the action right into the room. Clients are mobilized to confront the emergencies of their lives by playing out their aborted feelings and actions in relative safety. Talking about a situation is changed into doing.

Anecdotes can set the relevant background for the enactment. By talking about tensions in his body Raymond initiates his experiment. Polster (1987) points out that a major portion of the information of therapy is derived from the stories that people tell. What is important is not the specifics but the person's perception of those specifics. A father who drinks heavily may have various effects on his children. They require different behavioural responses depending on their unique personalities.

The direction of the experiment changes as Raymond talks first about his lack of awareness of tensions in his body, then his desire to feel in control of himself by ignoring these messages, and finally his identification of becoming still in his body when his father got drunk. Later, Raymond begins a dialogue. He chooses not to assume the role of his father; rather, he stays with his own experience. At this point, Raymond takes charge. The therapist respects his decision and moves on to explore his feelings in the group. Raymond realizes that he can express them and, at the same time, be in control of himself. The experiment enables Raymond to relate directly to his father what has been for him an unresolved issue from his past.

VARIABLES OF AN EXPERIMENT

Zinker (1977) identifies ten variables which are involved at some stage of the process of experiment. These are:

1. Laying the groundwork;
2. Negotiating consensus between the therapist and the client;
3. Grading the work in terms of experienced difficulty for the client;
4. Surfacing the client's awareness;
5. Locating the client's energy;
6. Focusing energy and awareness towards the development of a theme;
7. Generating self-support for both client and therapist;
8. Choosing a particular experiment;
9. Enacting the experiment;
10. Debriefing the client.

Each of these variables will be considered briefly.

Laying the groundwork

The most important part of any therapy is the initial sessions, where good contact between the therapist and client is or is not formed. O'Leary (1986) found that, after the first two sessions, the degree of empathy is established. This lays the groundwork for all therapy. In a group situation the therapist must ensure that an understanding of the member's world exists before engaging in experiment. A valuable asset in this regard is fascination. Polster (1987) describes fascination in the following terms: 'With fluid absorption in everything he said to me, my mind ticked off freely . . . spontaneously tuned in to those therapeutic concerns he came with' (p. 142). Only in such an atmosphere can exploration of the client's world begin. Zinker (1977) points out that at this point it is important not to interrupt clients, but to allow them to develop the feelings and ideas which spontaneously arise in them, in order to fully understand what is in their minds.

Consensus

Consensus relates to the checking by the therapist that the person is willing to undertake the particular actions required in the experiment. This will be more or less formal, depending on the length and depth of the relationship between the therapist and the client.

Grading of the experiment

The therapist needs to choose an experiment with which the client feels comfortable. At a particular workshop one of the participants was Art. When I asked the group to draw what they felt at that moment, Art insisted that he was unable to draw. I sought an easier and less demanding task and invited him to draw anything he wished. When he told me that he had never done any drawing, I suggested that he scribble or draw lines at random. When the group reconvened after this activity, Art produced a lovely desert scene complete with cacti and far-off mountains. The significance of the example is that, for the majority, the task was a familiar one while for Art its novelty was unnerving; for him it was an experiment. The proposed activity had to be reduced to a level at which he was comfortable.

Awareness

The previous example is also an illustration of how the therapist can heighten the client's self-awareness. When therapists attend to the awareness of the client, they clarify what is going on for that person. When Art and I engaged in the initial exchange, it became apparent to me that he was seeking attention. As the group worked, I made sure that I turned my back and looked out of the window. My hypothesis was confirmed when Art approached and reiterated his position. I then gave him my support by returning with him to the group to confirm him in this undertaking. I explored with him what he liked best. He replied the desert. We then investigated what appealed to him in the desert. He maintained that he could not draw it. At this point I suggested that he scribble or draw lines. I then returned to the window. I felt fairly certain that Art would empower himself once he had obtained a certain level of support from me. Further dialogue, I felt, would only aid him to maintain his 'I can't' position.

Energy

Zinker (1977) points out that an experiment will have a tendency to drag if the only source of energy is that of the therapist. In the example above, it was essential that Art make the decision to draw for himself. Allowing him both the time and space to do this was important, so that he mobilized his own resources.

Focusing energy and awareness towards the development of a theme

During a therapy session, the client may present several issues. It is important for the therapist and client to focus on one theme if a learning experience is to occur. For example, Muriel says that she feels confused because her best friend did not invite her to join her in a shopping outing and she does not know why. She also feels rejected because she was not asked to organize the ladies' outing as she had done last year. Furthermore her niece did not come to stay with her for a week's holidays, as had been planned.

Though the focus changed within a few minutes of therapy it became clear that a theme of 'rejection' had developed. The next step in the process was to help Muriel to become aware of this. Energy was generated by inviting Muriel to assume the posture of a rejected person. She moved to the corner of the room, sighed heavily and sat down. The therapist gave her a piece of cardboard and a marker and asked her to write an appropriate message. She wrote 'No one wants me'.

Generating self-support for both client and therapist

Establishing self-support in therapy may be likened to certain practices in sport. Have you ever watched golfers prepare for a tee-off? They establish conditions both in their bodies and in the environment which support them. Likewise when therapists work with clients, they tune in to both of these aspects. They make the necessary adjustments until they feel grounded in the room and are really present to the clients.

Having supported themselves, therapists ask clients to become grounded by a variety of methods, which include awareness of their breathing and bodily sensations. In dealing with Muriel, the therapist asked her to stand, support herself firmly and breathe deeply before continuing to work on the rejection theme.

Choosing a particular experiment

Creative therapists have an endless supply of experiments from which to draw. It is important that they select the one which is most appropriate for a particular client.

On continuing to work with Muriel, the therapist asked her to set up a dialogue between one of the people who had rejected her and herself. She chose to work on her niece. Ascertaining that dialogue work was the best method in which to engage with Muriel was an important aspect of the process.

Enacting the experiment

Having decided on dialogue as the most appropriate method, Muriel imagines a possible conversation between her niece and herself.

Therapist:	'Muriel, would you like to tell Eileen how you feel about the fact that she has decided not to visit you and stay for a while.'
Muriel:	'I feel hurt . . . disappointed . . . not good enough . . . I am wondering why you rejected me . . . What did I do that made you change your plans?'
Eileen:	'Aunt Muriel, I never meant to hurt you. You see, the girls I go around with decided to go camping because the weather was so fine. We had not planned it in advance, and I was sure you would not mind if I cancelled my holiday with you.'
Muriel:	'I had been looking forward to your coming . . . What did I do to you last summer that made you keep away?'
Eileen:	'You did nothing . . . I intended coming but this camping trip came up very unexpectedly.'
Therapist:	'Tell Eileen how you feel.'
Muriel:	'I feel passed over . . . I feel rejected.'

Having spent a while working on the rejection the dialogue continued.

Therapist: 'What does Eileen say to you now?'
Eileen: 'Aunt Muriel, I do not reject you. I love being in your
home. I will spend a while with you before school reopens.

Enacting the experiment enables Muriel to work through her hurt and to consider other aspects of her niece's behaviour which she had not heretofore considered.

Debriefing the client

Therapists do not assume what clients learn from an experiment; instead they ask them. Sometimes clients need time to absorb the experience.

Having worked on the rejection issue, Muriel was asked what the experiment meant to her. She said that she gradually realized that she misinterprets situations and makes assumptions about others' motives that are inaccurate.

FORMS OF AN EXPERIMENT

An experiment can take many forms and depends to a large extent on the creativity of the therapist. We will consider six of the more frequently used methods – the empty chair; playing the projection; rehearsal techniques; destroying the introject; reversal techniques; and undoing retroflections.

The empty chair

Use of the empty chair occurs in many forms of experiment: it is one of the best known and most widely used of the gestalt techniques. Fagan *et al.* (1974) outline some general principles when working with the empty chair. These are:

1. Do not begin until you have had personal experience of this procedure as a patient.
2. Be ready for explosions or strong emotional responses.
3. Until you are experienced in empty-chair work and/or know the patient well, be sure that you can provide adequate follow-up support and that the patient is emotionally stable.
4. As long as the process is moving, keep the therapeutic role to a minimum.
5. Move as gently as possible through impasses. If in doubt, do too little rather than going for a big breakthrough.
6. If confused about what the person is saying or doing, find out before doing anything else.

7. Given adequate safeguards, experiment and follow your own experience.

The empty chair is used to clarify both sides of an interaction. Clients switch back and forth from their own place to the empty chair. The dialogue usually relates to two polarized parts of the individual. Two possibilities arise when polarities are identified: they can either complement each other and lead to integration, or they can compete and isolate each other. As one side of the polarity makes contact with its opposite, a reorganization takes place within the person. The end goal is not to blend the two components into a grey composition, but rather, as Polster and Polster (1973) indicate, to let each emerge, depending on the situation at hand. The therapist ensures that each element expresses itself, stating its needs and wishes. The essential aspect of this work is the genuine expression of each part affirming its own precise identity. As the polarity becomes more defined, the client becomes more aware of the needs of both sides. Establishing contact between them can often result in extreme behaviour, for example, individuals who must scream their rage to counteract their submissiveness. In this instance, one part of the polarity has been frozen into inactivity. Its release can consequently be explosive in nature and the overstimulation can be expressed in crying, screaming, temper tantrums. Hence individuals may become temporarily difficult to live with while playing out the other side of their personalities. The therapist has to have faith in the self-regulation of clients, which is implicit in gestalt therapy.

James and Jongeward (1971) suggest using the empty chair technique in the following manner when dealing with anger:

1. Imagine the person who bothers you sitting opposite you. You say aloud how angry you are and why.
2. Become aware of your body's response to your anger. Do you restrict or hold back your anger with some part of your body? Do you clench your teeth or fist or colon? Exaggerate your restriction. Now what do you discover?
3. When you feel ready, reverse your roles and be that person. Respond as if the other is really present.
4. Continue the dialogue, switching back and forth.
5. If you find a phrase that fits or feels good, such as 'Stop embarrassing me' and 'Why didn't you protect me?', repeat the phrase several times, each time louder and louder until you are actually shouting.
6. Next, stand on a sturdy stool. Imagine that the person toward whom you feel anger is cowering beneath you.
7. Look down at this person and state what you are angry about and why. Say all the things you have always wanted to say and never dared.
8. If you feel like changing positions, do it.

Playing the projection

Projectors speak frequently of 'it' and 'them', and place responsibility for their actions outside themselves; they rarely deal in the authentic 'I' mode. Despite their attempts to foist their feelings on others, their unwanted feelings remain as personal baggage. Perls, Hefferline and Goodman (1951) point out that the only way to get rid of an undesired emotion is to accept it, express it and thus discharge it. They recommend that people go through a period in which their reaction to everything is 'that otherness is myself'. This is particularly true when they feel violent reactions of fear or passive helplessness. In this manner conversations which are usually full of what others did or wanted to do to them, are accepted as personal statements.

The first stage in undoing projection is to make 'I' statements. Individuals in a 'Poor little me' game who frequently say to themselves 'Nobody cares about me', are thus challenged to consider the possibility 'I care about nobody'. In this manner greater clarity between what is true of the surroundings and what is true of oneself can be established. Previously, the focus has exclusively been on the environment, in the sense of blaming it for life's circumstances.

Perls, Hefferline and Goodman (1951) give a somewhat humorous account of how to attend to 'it' expressions. They state: 'If you say "A thought struck me" just where and how did it strike? Did it use a weapon? Whom did you want to strike at the time? If you say "My heart aches" are you aching for something with all your heart? If you say "I have a headache", are you contracting your muscles so that you hurt your head?' (p. 216). In this manner, an awareness of projections may begin.

The most potent method of reowning projections, however, is to play them in a group situation. The next example illustrates this process.

Example: playing the projection

Clare:	'Dick is very controlling. He tells me only what suits him; otherwise he pretends to forget.'
Group Leader:	'Can you see Dick?' (Pause). 'What does he look like?'
Clare:	'Well he is tall, brown-eyed and good looking.'
Group Leader:	'Could you be Dick and tell Clare how you are?' (Brings empty chair in front of Clare).
Clare (as Dick):	'Well, Clare, I laugh inside when I see how gullible you are. You believe me when I tell you I forget. How could a successful businessman like me forget as frequently as I do? I like being free of you so I keep everything hazy. I do not want to be tied down by anyone.'

Group Leader:	'Would you now like to be Clare in this chair (pointing to other chair), and tell Dick how you feel about this.'
Clare:	'I am really angry' (clenches hands).
Group Leader:	'What are your hands doing?'
Clare:	'They want to hit Dick. I want to hit you Dick. You make me furious.'
Group Leader:	'What about saying "I make myself furious"?'
Clare:	'But I do not. He does it to me.'
Group Leader:	'Is Dick here right now?'
Clare:	'No.' (Pauses. Long silence). 'I guess I make myself furious.'
Group Leader:	'You guess it?'
Clare:	'I make myself furious.'
Group Leader:	'Would you like to tell Dick that?'
Clare:	'I make myself furious. I know that you are pretending to forget. I am not gullible.'
Group Leader:	'Tell Dick what you want.'
Clare:	'I want you to remember dates and times! Oh! It has just occurred to me that I am trying to control Dick as well.'

In this example, role reversal enables Clare to see that she is trying to control Dick. Discovered similarity between persons can contribute to mutual understanding, especially when the relationship has been based on imagined or assumed differences. Role reversal enables Clare to contact parts of herself that have long been denied.

Rehearsal techniques

Gestalt therapists often use 'rehearsal' techniques so that clients may model reactions to experiences with which they have difficulty. It involves reliving a situation in the 'now' in the manner in which individuals originally reacted. Following this they work on facets which they felt were inappropriate and unsatisfactory. Finally, new modes of action are put into practice through rehearsal. This provides the level of encouragement necessary to deal with the emotions which emerge. They then attempt the same in a less supportive situation outside therapy.

Example: rehearsal techniques

Beverly:	'I hate going to cocktail parties related to my husband's business. I just stand there and feel dumb. I keep thinking "Why can't I think of something to say?" It is difficult for Dan too since he keeps

	checking with me non-verbally across the room to see how I am coping.'
Group Facilitator:	'What exactly do you do?'
Beverly:	'I go up to someone and say "Hello, I am Beverly McMullen". The other person replies "I am John Smith. Which department do you work in?" I say "I am Dan McMullen's wife" and then somehow we just look at each other and I get more and more uncomfortable until John Smith excuses himself saying he has to speak to Harry Shlien.'
Group Facilitator:	'Okay. Could we use the group to relive the situation?'
Beverly:	'Fine.' (The group stand around as if at a cocktail party).
Group Facilitator:	(to Beverly) 'Could you now act as if you are at the party?'
Beverly:	(to one group of three) 'Hello I am Beverly McMullen.' Group respond "Hello Beverly", and continue conversation.
Group Facilitator:	'What are you feeling now Beverly?'
Beverly:	'Just as at the cocktail party, I am feeling out of it since they are talking about work.'
Group Facilitator:	'What can you do to feel part of it?'
Beverly:	'I do not know.' (Pause) 'Well, I suppose since they are talking about personnel, I could ask them about absenteeism.'
Group Facilitator:	'You suppose.'
Beverly:	'Well, I can' (turns to group of three). 'What is your rate of absenteeism?' (One person from group answers). 'I have realized that I can ask questions. I do not have to know about the job.'

In this rehearsal Beverly discovers that she can ask questions to include herself in the group and to avoid feeling left out. She also finds that her reaction is the same in the supportive and trusting group environment as at the cocktail party. When the group facilitator enquires 'What can you do to feel part of it?' her energy is mobilized to find her own solutions. Murgatroyd (1985) indicates that the intention is not to develop and refine some specific behaviours, but rather in working primarily with feelings, the idea is to minimize the use of routine and to encourage spontaneity. The rehearsal invites individuals to explore themselves and to become responsible. It can be particularly useful if the person is apprehensive about dealing with some situation in the future, such as going for a job interview or job promotion.

Destroying the introject

In Chapter 3 the injunction 'Never trust anyone' was given as an example of an introject. In the following example, Kristen becomes aware of how she has introjected her mother's admonition never to trust anyone.

Kristen:	'I feel I do not trust George. He has asked can he come and stay for a week of the holidays but I say to myself why did he never come when I was in Iowa. New York is such a convenient place for him.'
Group Facilitator:	'So you feel that George may be using you?'
Kristen:	'Yes – although we have had good conversations when we did the same postgraduate course.'
Group Facilitator:	'How bad is it if he is using you?'
Kristen:	'Well, it relates to my never trusting anyone. If that is what he is doing and I discover it, I will say to myself, "Never trust anyone".'
Group Facilitator:	'So he will confirm what you already know.'
Kristen:	'Yes. I had not thought of it that way. But it is a problem for me – trusting I mean.'
Group Facilitator:	'When you say to yourself "Never trust anyone" whose voice do you hear?'
Kristen:	'Whose voice do I hear? My own of course. Wait a minute. My mother always said that to me.'
Group Facilitator:	'Your mother always said "Never trust anyone".'
Kristen:	'Well, never trust men in particular. Men are after only one thing she used to say.'
Group Facilitator:	'Would you like to be your mother seated here in this chair (points to empty chair) and tell Kristen never to trust men.'
Kristen (as mother):	'Kristen never trust men. They are selfish creatures, out for what they can get for themselves. Do not let them fool you or trick you.'
Group Facilitator:	'Could you be Kristen (points to empty chair) and respond to her?'
Kristen:	'Mother, that is not true. Only some men are selfish. I have listened to you for too long. You have destroyed my life. I hate you!'
Group Facilitator:	'What is going on for you Kristen?'
Kristen:	'I feel sick in my stomach.'
Group Facilitator:	'If your stomach could speak what would it say?'
Kristen:	'I hate you Mother. You have destroyed me.'
Group Facilitator:	'Your mother has destroyed your life?'

Kristen:	'Well, I have allowed her to do so by listening to her.'
Group Facilitator:	'What do you need to say to her?'
Kristen:	'Mother, I have been lonely and isolated. I have done what you told me and where has it got me? Here I am at 35, single and without any significant male relationship in my life. I am not going to listen to you any longer. I am going to say 'yes' to George's request to come and stay for a week. I will not prejudge the situation. I will wait and see.'

In this example Kristen had swallowed the introject 'never trust anyone' wholly. Thereafter she was tortured by the loneliness and frustration of such a life situation. Perls, Hefferline and Goodman (1951) state that introjectors move the boundary between themselves and the rest of the world so far inside themselves that there is almost nothing of themselves left!

The use of the empty chair allowed Kristen to externalize the introject viz. 'Never trust anyone'. Kristen had incorporated this aspect of her mother into her system. By placing her mother in the empty chair she became aware of the origin of her introject. Further, by engaging in a dialogue with her, the introject was able to surface clearly and she fully experienced the conflict. Central to this work was Kristen's ability to differentiate between what for her was 'me' and 'not me'. She became aware of her own stored-up bitterness. However, the therapist enabled her to work through the bitterness and to experience the aggression. Only through aggression was the introject destroyed. In Kristen's case the feeling of bitterness ('You have destroyed my life') was followed very rapidly by aggression – 'I hate you! I hate you!' Polster and Polster (1973) point out that original changes may be at random, with individuals not really knowing what they want. Still, they are important as they allow clients to see what they do not desire. In Kristen's case, she expresses what she does not want in 'I am not going to listen to you any longer'.

As Kristen worked on the introject from her mother 'Never trust anyone', she felt sick in her stomach. This is a frequent reaction. People who are introjectors have taken in something which has not been assimilated as part of themselves; it is a foreign body and has to be dislodged. In the process the person may actually be physically sick. Perls, Hefferline and Goodman (1951) used the activity of eating as a way of becoming aware of introjects. They state: 'Forced feeding, forced education, forced mortality, forced identifications with parents and siblings, result in literally thousands of unassimilated odds and ends lodged in the psychosomatic organism as introjects. They are both undigested and, as they stand, indigestible. Men and women, long accustomed to being resigned to 'the way things are', continue to hold their noses, desensitize their palates, and swallow down still more' (p. 202).

A trainee in a gestalt therapy programme describes her experience in following some of the exercises outlined by Perls, Hefferline and Goodman (1951). Initially she felt resistance to eating slowly, but she persevered. She goes on to say, 'I am glad that I did. Through these exercises, I became far more aware of values I had introjected. "Shoulds" often hit me out of the blue and I examined them. Some I chose to disregard, e.g. "You should never be late for anything", "Allow yourself 10 minutes to spare". Working at some of my "shoulds" has freed me but there are more introjects to be vomited up for dislodgement or assimilation'.

At another point she wrote 'Through eating experiments over the last few months I have become much more aware of my introjects. This did not happen overnight but after a long time the "Aha" moment occurred. After four to five weeks, I was finishing lunch at my mother's house. Mam offered me more vegetables, the peas and carrots which she had grown especially in her garden for me! I agreed to have more "Just to please you!" At that moment I became very much aware that I had been swallowing not just physical food but a lot of her values and attitudes "just to please" her. This was a huge breakthrough and since then several introjects have surfaced for me'.

Reversal techniques

Reversal techniques allow individuals to display behaviour opposite to that which they normally exhibit. The timid can be asked to speak in a loud voice to other group members. Take the case of Susan, the police drill inspector, who while speaking could scarcely be heard. The facilitator invited her to stand in front of the group and to pretend that they were police trainees. She was to speak to them in the voice she normally used in the barracks. When Susan had performed this task, the group facilitator checked with her what was happening for her. It emerged that she remembered her mother's voice saying 'Ladies should be seen and not heard'.

Undoing retroflections

To undo retroflections, individuals must become aware of them. Body awareness leads to mobilization of the repressed energy which has been invested in the retroflection. Action ensues. However, clients may experience strong resistance to this reversal process, since it attacks the coping mechanisms they have built for themselves.

One of the most common retroflections is stroking or hugging oneself, which usually indicates a need to be comforted. Perls, Hefferline and Goodman (1951) state that the 'treatment of retroflection is simple, merely reverse the direction of the retroflecting act from inward to outward' (p. 148). However, the first step is to discover the retroflection. As awareness develops, previously blocked impulses are expressed appropriately. Hence persons who heretofore hugged themselves now hug others, or invite others to hug them.

Zinker (1977) points out that retroflectors usually suffer physical (musculoskeletal) symptoms which show where the energy is frozen. Tension in the neck, shoulders and arms may reflect an interruption of needs involving contact with others, such as holding, hugging, hitting. In undoing retroflections, the therapist seeks to bridge blockages between awareness and energy.

Another example of retroflection is when clients hit themselves. The solution lies in the discharge of the anger which hitherto has been repressed inwards, rather than pushed outwards on to the environment. Perls, Hefferline and Goodman (1951) recommend: 'When you discover an impulse to do something, which cannot reasonably in its primitive form find a direct expression, do not turn it back against yourself, turn it against any kind of object that is convenient' (p. 177). The following materials are particularly useful in the discharging of anger – pillows, towels, punchbags, tennis rackets. Rosenblatt (1976) recommends that individuals pound, strangle, throttle or garrotte the pillow, while screaming at the same time if desired. This results in feelings of strength, power, excitement and refreshment, as the energy previously used in controlling the anger is now released and the blocked energy flows.

A powerful method of freeing anger is for clients to imagine the person(s) with whom they are angry in front of them. The following story is an interesting example of how to deal with unfinished anger: the retired first mate of an English merchant ship used to give a penny each morning to a boy on his way to school, for doing the following: the boy knocked on the door and on entering said 'The captain wants you immediately'. The old tar would reply in a loud and angry voice 'Tell the captain to go to hell'.

Chapter 6

Dreams and fantasies

DREAMS

As a psychoanalyst it was not surprising that Perls (1975) paid attention to dreams. Indeed, his book *Gestalt therapy verbatim* (1969b) deals exclusively with the subject. Freud (1900) may be regarded as the pioneer of the exploration of dreams. He stressed their importance, believing that they were the royal road to the unconscious. In dreams, he claimed, unconscious material which might disturb sleep is changed into symbols that are acceptable to the conscious ego, and that can be tolerated without emotional disturbance. The transformation of this unconscious material is called the 'dream work'. The symbolism itself involves the representation of unconscious material without revealing its real meaning in consciousness. The latent content of dreams cannot be brought to consciousness in an absolutely undisguised form; rather, it must be expressed in words or other symbols which can be understood by analyst and patient together. In turn these are interpreted so that the emotional tensions associated in the dream are discharged, and the childhood experiences are proved harmless and integrated into adult life.

Whereas Freud (1975) called the dream the royal road to the unconscious, Perls (1969b) viewed it as the royal road to integration. The dream is the most spontaneous expression of the existence of the human being. With most things in life, a person has some kind of control; not so with the dream. Its different parts are fragments of personality, some of which have been disowned. Perls (1969b) believed that in a dream we have a clear existential message of what is missing in our lives, what we avoid doing and living. Page (1984) says of dreams: 'The experience is unique to the person, whether it is frustrating, frightening, boring or beautiful' (p. 196).

Perls (1969b) also emphasized the dream as a projection, where wishes, attitudes and behaviour are attributed to someone other than one's own self. Parts of the personality have been fragmented and projected on to others. In working through the dream these are reowned. Perls believed that clients should play all the parts in order to identify disowned projections. They are often accompanied by a feeling of alienation: 'That's not me, that's something else, something not belonging to me'. The therapist sometimes encounters an unwillingness to work with alienated parts. This is not surprising, since individuals have rejected these aspects of personality, and because of this they are impoverished. The dream allows them to rediscover that which they have lost.

In gestalt therapy, no interpreting of the dream or symbolism is used or recognized as valid. The dream is unfinished business from the person's life, and a statement of the here-and-now existence of the dreamer. The person is invited to re-experience the dream by telling it aloud in the present tense. Every detail is part of the life of the dreamer. The client is all the people, things, places and actions in the dream. The therapist uses a guided imagery associative process through inviting the individual to animate the dream and to give voices to the people and objects. The timespan which has elapsed since the dream occurred is of no consequence. The fact that it is remembered means that is is unfinished business in the life of the individual.

The most important dreams are recurring ones. Their reoccurrence indicates that a gestalt has not been closed; there is a problem or difficulty which has not been completed and cannot recede into the background. Dreams are a means of re-experiencing and working through emotionally charged experiences. They may reoccur but the form will have changed, encompassing that part of the experience with which the dreamer has dealt.

If individuals are unable to remember their dreams, James and Jongeward (1971) recommend that they keep a pencil and paper by the bedside and write down the dream immediately upon waking. Perls (1969b) advised: 'Write the dream down and make a list of all the details in the dream. Get every person, every thing, every mood, and then work on these to become each one of them' (p. 74). He recommended that when individuals started to work on a dream they should note where it was occurring. The environment in which the dream occurs provides the background.

In dream work the gestalt therapist invites the client to become a person or element in the dream and to state what comes to mind. Since everything in the dream reflects aspects of the person, learning can occur from any part of it. Perls (1969b) stated that he let the client play all the aspects of the dream because only through doing this can the person get the full identification of what is going on. Individuals will have most difficulty in playing the disowned or alienated part, since they do not want to reown it. In this manner they get a clearer picture of what they are rejecting.

Various possibilities exist for working with the dream. The first starts with the 'I' element. Clients can be themselves in the dream and speak in the first person. The second option is to begin with the person or object in which clients are most interested. Thirdly, clients can begin with the person or object they find most difficult to remember, or that which they regard as most alien to themselves.

In working with dialogue, various approaches may be used. Clients can be themselves and talk to other people or objects in the dream, and let them respond. If there is a problem in the dream, the empty chair can represent it: clients can be invited to conduct a dialogue with the problem in this manner. There may be a dialogue between two people in the dream; alternatively, the dialogue can be between a person and an object, or between an object and an object. If the dialogue breaks down, it is important for the therapist to ask the client 'What is going on for you now?' In this way, the therapist does not intervene too rapidly but allows clients the opportunity to discover for themselves what is happening.

In working with dreams therapists may deal with a small part, since awareness can be greatly enhanced even from a portion. Each stage of dream work increases assimilation. As clients work on the dream, it will change and the existential message will become clearer. Perls (1969b) stated that he used to work through all parts of the dream, but then he began to look for 'holes, emptiness, stuckness and avoidances'. When clients get into the vicinity of holes they become confused or nervous. This, Perls believed, was the impasse which they tend to avoid. The role of the therapist is to support them to confront what they are rejecting.

Rainwater (1976) offers a slightly different approach to working with dreams. She suggests the following:

1. Identify with any mysterious object, such as an unopened letter or an unread book.
2. Be the landscape or the environment.
3. Be anything that is missing in the dream. If you do not remember your dreams, then speak to your missing dreams.
4. Be alert for any numbers that appear in the dream. Become these numbers and explore the associations with them.
5. Be any objects that link or join, such as telephone lines and highways.
6. Become all the people in the dream. Are any of them significant people?
7. Assume the identity of any powerful force.
8. Become any two contrasting objects.

Rainwater (1976) advises that the dreamer notice the feeling of the dream: identifying the feeling tone may be the key to finding its meaning. Dreamers can focus on questions such as:

- What are you feeling?
- What are you doing in the dream?
- What do you want in the dream?
- What are your relationships with other objects and people in the dream?
- What kind of action can you take now?
- What is your dream telling you?

Although Perls (1969b) preferred to view the dream as a projection and to concentrate on playing the various persons and objects in it, he also emphasized contact. He frequently asked the dreamer to repeat part of the dream and to tell it to either one or more members in the group. He emphasized the interpersonal dynamic between the therapist and dreamer by sharing his own perceptions. The empty chair provided the person with the opportunity to come into contact with the external target of the dream. It also forced dreamers to get in touch with their aggressiveness, to become it rather than to intellectualize or talk about it.

In the same vein, Polster and Polster (1973) view the dream primarily in the context of contact, and set up dialogues between the different parts. The dream, they believe, holds generative power in unfolding interaction between the dreamer and therapist, or dreamer and group members. It can be used as a starting point to discover present relationships with other group members, or with the therapist. It can recognize an existential position which requires exploration, using the dream only as a point of departure. Take, for example, Kate, who in identifying the feeling tone of the dream feels isolated and alone. The therapist can, in this instance, invite her to look around the room and consider how she feels isolated and alone in the group. In this manner the isolation and aloneness which are the existential message of the dream can be worked through in the immediacy and interaction of the group situation. Polster and Polster state: 'The dream workthrough in one sense may thus never actually return to the dream itself, but rather responds to its existential message about the person's life' (p. 274).

The individual's experience of the group has been used by Zinker (1977) to create group experiments. The sequence in this particular approach is as follows:

1. The dream is reported by the client and it is worked through on an individual level.
2. The dream is then developed into a group experience where members play out the various parts. The dreamer selects group members to play these parts or they can volunteer to do so.
3. The dreamer directs the group in developing the dream. Alternatively, he gives them free rein and becomes aware of how others experience the qualities he encountered in the dream.

This approach offers the group members a range of opportunities for enacting a facet of the dream which may relate not only to the dreamer but also to their own lives. Zinker's (1977) assumption is that all people share themes. Images within the group are selectively appealing to various group members, and may be used to enhance understanding of themselves within the group process. This approach, Zinker points out, incorporates group participants, as opposed to the observational role to which group members are usually relegated. On the negative side, it closely resembles the approach of psychodrama, wherein projections and interpretations occur. The dream is seen from the outside rather than from within.

The following is a transcript of Kate's recurring dream. Having asked her to ground herself and to get in touch with her breathing, the therapist invites her to tell her dream in the present tense:

Kate: 'I am in a house, a room really . . . It is a cabin . . . a one-roomed house . . . small and cold . . . Very cold . . . The walls are bare, without plaster or paper . . . or paint. The floor is cold . . . and . . . bare . . . and the window is very small – tiny . . . just about 8 inches by a foot. There are no curtains on it but the glass is covered with . . . thick, thick cobwebs. They are all over the place, . . . all over the house. It is so dusty. Where the fireplace is . . . there is just the hearth and cobwebs all round it . . . Just cobwebs everywhere . . . That is the dream.'

Therapist: 'Alright Kate. I want you to become the cobwebs now and to speak as the cobwebs.'

Kate: 'Well the cobwebs are thick and they are just about everywhere.'

Therapist: 'I want you to actually become the cobwebs. If they could speak, what would they say?'

Kate: 'Oh yes! We are cobwebs . . . and we are covering this house, this cabin . . . We are on the walls . . . on the floor . . . on the hearth . . . We are hanging from the ceiling . . . We are covering the windows.'

Therapist: 'Now I want you to become the cabin and to speak as it.'

Kate: 'The cabin is small and cold . . . No one lives in it anymore . . .'

Therapist: 'One second Kate. Speak as the cabin, not about it, just as you did for the cobwebs.'

Kate: 'Right. I am a small, cold cabin . . . I am deserted . . . no-one lives here any more. I am smothered with dust and cobwebs . . . I am just left . . . to . . . fall down . . . No light can get in to me because . . . the cobwebs . . . they block out the sun . . .'

Therapist: 'Did you notice the difference in your voice between the time you spoke as the cobwebs and when you were the cabin?'

Kate: 'I sounded real weak as the cabin.'

Therapist:	'And I heard strength and power in the cobwebs.'
Kate:	'Yes! they are stronger by far.'
Therapist:	'Now I want you to do a dialogue between the cabin and the cobwebs.'
Kate:	'The chair thing?'
Therapist:	'Yes. Will you try it?'
Kate:	'Yes!'
Therapist:	'Arrange the two chairs as you want to have them.' (Kate places the two chairs facing each other and sits in one herself).
Therapist:	'Can you feel the floor under you?'
Kate:	'No, not really.'
Therapist:	'Take a few minutes to ground yourself . . . and become aware of your breathing. When you feel ready to start the dialogue, go ahead.' (Kate spends a few minutes grounding herself.)
Kate:	'I will start as the cobwebs.'
Therapist:	'Fine.'
Kate:	'We are really powerful cobwebs and though we appear flimsy, the dust has reinforced us and we have become as strong as nylon . . . like elastic curtains. No one can sweep us away . . .'
Therapist:	'Answer back as the cabin.' (Kate changes chairs.)
Kate:	'I know you are very strong . . .'
Therapist:	'What else does the cabin say?'
Kate:	'Nothing . . .'
Therapist:	'What about the cobwebs?' (Kate changes chairs.)
Kate:	'We are stronger than you, much stronger . . .'
Therapist:	'Answer back as the cabin.' (Kate changes chairs.)
Therapist:	'You have just heard the cobwebs say how strong they are, they are stronger than you. Has the cabin any response to make to that?'
Kate:	'Yes, you are stronger than me . . .'
Therapist:	'Yes, you are stronger than me . . .'
Therapist:	'Does the cabin have anything else to say?'
Kate:	'No . . .'
Therapist:	'Be the cobwebs again.'
Kate:	(Changes chairs). 'We are ruling this place. We have taken over. We are mighty.'
Therapist:	'What does the cabin answer?' (Kate changes chairs.)
Kate:	'Yes, you have and you are only cobwebs . . . I am made of stone but I am choked by you. You are ruining me.'

Therapist:	'What are you feeling right now Kate?'
Kate:	'I feel . . . so sad . . . so helpless.'
Therapist:	'I want you to stay in touch with that sadness for a while . . . What does it feel like?'
Kate:	'I feel . . . isolated . . . and . . . cold . . . and all alone.'
Therapist:	'Just like the cabin?'
Kate:	'Exactly like the cabin. That cabin is a symbol of me.'
Therapist:	'Say that again Kate.'
Kate:	(No reply).
Therapist:	'What is going on for you Kate?'
Kate:	'I have been . . . describing myself all along . . . I see it clearly now . . . that cabin is me and I feel so sad.'
Therapist:	'Tell me about the sadness.'
Kate:	'I feel so alone.' (She swallows and blocks tears.)
Therapist:	'Kate, do not hold back those tears.'
Kate:	'I . . . I . . . never cry.'
Therapist:	'It is alright to cry here.'
Kate:	'Oh, I feel . . . so alone.' (Tears fill her eyes again.)
Therapist:	'Let the tears flow . . . Do not hold them back Kate . . . Let out the sound . . . Let out the sadness.' (Kate sobs for some time, making audible sounds.)
Kate:	'I feel foolish crying.'
Therapist:	'Who said it is foolish to cry?'
Kate:	'No one really . . . It is just . . . that I never cry.'
Therapist:	'And how does it feel to have cried just now?'
Kate:	'Well, I feel . . . relieved really . . . but there is a lot of things still there.'
Therapist:	'What are those things?'
Kate:	'Well I am focusing . . . on the table.'
Therapist:	'You did not mention that a while ago.'
Kate:	'Yes . . . I know . . . I did not think it was important . . . but maybe it is.'
Therapist:	'What is significant about the table?'
Kate:	'Well . . . I want to and I do not want to look at it . . it is the message really . . . I am afraid of looking at it.'
Therapist:	'What is the message?'
Kate:	'I am stuck here.'
Therapist:	'Could you describe the stuckness?'
Kate:	(No reply).
Therapist:	'Where are you stuck?'
Kate:	'I am stuck . . . at the message and the table.'
Therapist:	'What kind of table is it?'

Kate:	'Oh, it is really out of place, because it is a beautiful table like mahogany and it is exquisitely carved . . . but . . . it is covered with cobwebs again.'
Therapist:	'Will you become the table and speak to those cobwebs?'
Kate:	'I am a treasure in this cabin but . . . no one bothers to come to see me . . . because the cobwebs are covering me.'
Therapist:	'Speak to the cobwebs . . . Because you are covering me.'
Kate:	'Because you are covering me and my beauty and elegance is hidden.'
Therapist:	'Kate, repeat that last sentence.'
Kate:	'My beauty and elegance is hidden.'
Therapist:	'Say it again.'
Kate:	'My beauty and elegance is hidden.'
Therapist:	'How are you feeling now?'
Kate:	'I feel sad because I know this is true.'
Therapist:	'How are you hiding your beauty and elegance?'
Kate:	'It is all this sadness.'
Therapist:	'What sadness Kate?'
Kate:	'Well . . . it is coming from the message.'
Therapist:	'The message.'
Kate:	'The message in the dream.' (She covers her eyes with her hands.)
Therapist:	'What are your hands doing?'
Kate:	'Covering my eyes.'
Therapist:	'What are you avoiding looking at?'
Kate:	'The message.'
Therapist:	'And it says . . .'
Kate:	'No one cares.'
Therapist:	'Repeat that message.'
Kate:	'No one cares.'
Therapist:	'Say it again.'
Kate:	'No one cares . . . and it is true' (she begins to cry).
Therapist:	'Let yourself cry . . . let out the sadness.' (Kate cries for a while.) 'What are you feeling now Kate?'
Kate:	'I do not know . . . I feel confused.'
Therapist:	'What are you doing with your hands?' (Her hands are moving in a pushing movement.)
Kate:	'I do not know.'
Therapist:	'Exaggerate the movement.' (Kate does so.)
Kate:	'I am trying to push away all the confusion . . . and get rid of it.'
Therapist:	'Stay with the confusion Kate.'
Kate:	'. . . I am confused, I am so confused . . . it is the message.'

Therapist:	'You avoided looking at the message for a long time.'
Kate:	'It is too painful.'
Therapist:	'That no one cares.'
Kate:	'That no one cares.'
Therapist:	'Is that true?'
Kate:	'Yes.'
Therapist:	'I want you to say "No one cares" a few times.' (Kate does so). 'What are you feeling now?'
Kate:	'It is not fully true I suppose.'
Therapist:	'You suppose.'
Kate:	'Yes, I suppose some people do care . . .'
Therapist:	'I want you to change the "I suppose" to "I know".'
Kate:	'I know some people care about me.'
Therapist:	'Is that true?'
Kate:	'It is.'
Therapist:	'Can you name them?'
Kate:	'Well, I suppose Mum and Dad care.'
Therapist:	'Do you know it or do you just suppose it?'
Kate:	'I know it.'
Therapist:	'You know it.'
Kate:	'I know Mum and Dad care about me.'
Therapist:	'Anyone else?'
Kate:	'Well . . . Sheila does . . . and Kay . . . and you do.'
Therapist:	'I do Kate, you are right . . . any others?'
Kate:	'I am not sure of others to be honest.'
Therapist:	'I want you to give me a clear statement telling me about the people who really care about you.'
Kate:	'I know Mum and Dad and Sheila and yourself and Kay really care about me.'
Therapist:	'How do you feel now, having said that?'
Kate:	'I feel much stronger.'
Therapist:	'I want you to stay with that feeling for a few minutes.' (Kate does so.)
Kate:	'Yes, it is good, it is a strong feeling.'
Therapist:	'Could you make an "I" statement?'
Kate:	'I am good, . . . I am strong.'
Therapist:	'Stay with that feeling . . . Are you aware of what you are doing with your hands?'
Kate:	'I am . . . rubbing.'
Therapist:	'Rubbing what?'
Kate:	'It seems as if I am rubbing the message off the table.'
Therapist:	'It seems? Or are you actually rubbing?'
Kate:	'I am rubbing out the message.'

Therapist:	'Continue to make that rubbing movement . . . What are you feeling now?'
Kate:	'I have rubbed the message away – it is not true any more.'
Therapist:	'So what is true?'
Kate:	'There are people in my life who care about me.'
Therapist:	'You are certain?'
Kate:	'I am certain, I know it.'
Therapist:	'Kate . . . We are coming to the end of the session and I want you to get in touch with your breathing again . . . and become aware of your body . . . Now summarize for me what you have got from this session.'
Kate:	'Well, . . . the best thing is the strength I feel because I have identified the people who care for me.'
Therapist:	'Right.'
Kate:	'And I have cancelled the message that has been bugging me.'
Therapist:	'And you avoided it for a long time.'
Kate:	'Yes, I was afraid of what might come up . . . Yes, but I know I am not finished yet.'
Therapist:	'You can work on these at the next session'.
Kate:	'Yes, I will. I did not expect to cry . . . you would never think that there could have been so much in one dream.'

Because the dream was a recurring one the therapist knew that much unfinished business was contained within it. Difficulties in Kate's life emerged as the dream was recalled, and it was clear that she believed no one cared for her. There were a number of stages in the process.

In *stage one*, the therapist invited Kate to report the dream in the present tense. Her description was dominated by the presence of cobwebs.

In *stage two*, an invitation was given to become the cobwebs and speak as them. Kate experienced some difficulty in doing this. The therapist reiterated the instruction, which reassured Kate that she was to speak as the cobwebs. This technique of repeating the directions was again used when working on the cabin element.

In *stage three*, the therapist drew attention to the difference in the strength of Kate's voice when speaking as the cobwebs and as the cabin. This discrepancy served as an introduction to the ensuing dialogue.

Stage four began with the therapist's awareness that the client was not grounded. She then allowed the client the necessary space to ground herself, a procedure with which she was already familiar.

In *stage five*, the topdog/underdog split was reflected in the struggle between the cobwebs and the cabin. The therapist invited Kate to use the empty chair to enable her to differentiate more sharply between the two elements.

In *stage six*, the therapist explored the feeling tone of the dream by asking 'What are you feeling right now?' Kate identified feelings of sadness and alienation.

Stage seven. Kate had a script for herself that she never cried. The therapist gave her permission to do so by saying 'It is alright to cry here'. Kate reacted by allowing tears to flow. Subsequently the therapist investigated the origins of the script. When this did not yield any important information, she invited the client to consider the consequences of crying in the therapy situation. Having done so Kate discovered that she experienced a feeling of relief.

Stage eight marked an important progression in the work, when the therapist explored with Kate what she meant by 'there is a lot of things still there'. A less experienced individual may have focused on the feeling of relief and concluded the session. Instead the initial impasse associated with the table was overcome when the client was invited to describe it. Repetition was used to increase Kate's awareness of her hidden beauty and elegance. The feeling of sadness returned.

In *stage nine*, attention was focused on the client's non-verbal behaviour of covering her eyes with her hand. This resulted in the owning by Kate of her belief that no one cared for her. The therapist drew attention to Kate's pushing hand movement: this allowed her the opportunity to stay with rather than avoid the further exploration of her belief that no one cared.

In *stage ten*, repetition of the phrase 'no one cares' convinced Kate that the statement was not true, and she listed the people who did care. The therapist acknowledged and confirmed her own inclusion on that list. In checking her resultant feelings Kate experienced strength. Changing the 'it' nature of the statement allowed Kate to say of herself 'I am good . . . I am strong'.

In *stage eleven*, by adverting to the rubbing movement of her hands, the client realized that she had indeed finished with the belief that no one cared about her. The session concluded with the therapist inviting Kate to become aware of her breathing and to summarize what she had learnt from the session.

FANTASIES

Like dreams, fantasies are a valuable tool in therapy: they may be considered as waking dreams. Both fantasies and dreams are messages to the person that unfinished situations are calling for completion. In today's world there is little tolerance for fantasy, since it is often associated with hallucinations. However, it is encouraged in fairy tales. This ability is pushed aside at an early age in favour of the alphabet and cognitively oriented schooling. Fantasy is then viewed as a distraction. I remember my brother once receiving a comment on an English essay, 'Too much fantasy'.

Fantasy, however, is one of the richest avenues of escape available to the human being, in that it offers a temporary reprieve from reality, especially if that reality is boring, wearisome or frightening. When the more common procedures of group or indivdual therapy are not successful, it may be used to facilitate contact. The inability to make progress can be alleviated by using fantasy. Past events may be examined and future activities rehearsed.

Fantasies can be spontaneous reversals of experience. What we fantasize may be the reverse of a present frustration. For example, if we are sick we imagine what it would be like to be well and happy. If we study the content of our fantasies we can learn in what areas we feel frustrated. Through them individuals live out what they would prefer to be doing in life. Fantasies can be unhelpful only if they are indulged in frequently and crowd out real-life events.

Fantasy is highly related to creativity. Historically, the quest for new horizons has frequently been realized by allowing for the possibility of the fantastic. Exploring areas outside the realm of customary thinking can offer suggestions as to possible alternatives for the individual. Limits which have been experienced as real can be subjected to a new evaluation. Possibilities can become probabilities. Clarkson (1989) states that 'People need to begin to allow themselves to conceive of being different from the way they are. Thus a bridge is created between the current reality and the 'conceivable self'. Sometimes action starts in the head' (p. 106).

The use of fantasy in counselling is based on the difference between 'aboutism' and 'enactment'. When a client talks about an experience, facts are being chronicled or reported. Often they relate to past issues rather than dealing with present events. When enactment brings life to an occurrence, greater involvement occurs on the person's part, which enhances a sense of awareness and permits fresh discoveries. In his use of psychodrama, Moreno (1946) stressed that individuals are more likely to make discoveries by participating in an experience rather than by relating it. This emphasis acknoweldged the force of direct experience and moved therapy beyond reliance on the interpretive function so central to the psychoanalytic approach. When individuals identify with elements of fantasy they are associating closely with them, and much can be learned by them if they explore those elements. There is no limit to the number of objects with which they can identify. Individuals begin by describing physical characteristics, and as they move into the identification they begin to attribute their own characteristics to the different people or objects.

Fantasy enables individuals to forget the usual way they think about themselves. It can lead to valuable new learning. For example, repressed parts can be reclaimed. Stevens (1971) states: 'If you encounter unpleasantness in your fantasy experience, that does not mean that you are stuck with this unpleasantness for the rest of your life. It does mean that you have something unpleasant to deal with, something to work through and experience more fully' (p. 148).

Interaction among the various components can make the fantasy even richer in the discovery of identifications and projections. Limitations are subject only to the imagination and willingness of the subject. If a person is using dialogue for the first time, it may be more appropriate to 'write a script'. The client imagines two individuals or objects having a conversation, and identifies what each would say. In this instance, no attempt is made to conduct the dialogue in the present tense. As individuals become accustomed to this procedure, they can use the empty chair method to clarify and differentiate the sides of the dialogue. Differences in the client's posture and tone of voice are noticed as they move from one chair to another.

Therapist: 'Eileen, I want you to sit comfortably or lie on your back on the floor.' (Eileen chooses to sit). 'Close your eyes and become aware of your feet contacting the ground . . . and the chair supporting you.

Tune in to your body. How is it? . . . Become aware of your entire body from your toes to your head . . .

Be aware of any physical pain or tiredness or tension points . . .

Let go of any tight spots especially on your shoulders or neck or jaw . . .

Become aware of your breathing . . . Be aware of the air as it comes in and goes out through your nostrils . . . Do not control your breathing . . . just be aware of it as it is . . .

Now focus your attention on your thoughts or images . . . Let them pass through . . . Do not engage them . . . Imagine that they are birds escaping from an open cage, flying into the sky . . . away into the horizon and out of sight.

Become aware of your feelings about being here now and any other feelings that surface for you. Accept these feelings and let them be. Now I would like you to imagine that you are a TREE. Become this tree and describe yourself as the tree . . . "I am" –

What kind of tree are you? . . .

How are you rooted in the ground? . . . In what kind of soil do you grow?

What is your trunk like? . . .

What kind of bark do you have? . . .

What are your branches like? . . .

What season is it? . . . How do your branches look in this season? . . .

What happens at each season?

What are your surroundings like?

Is there anything else on or near you? . . .

How do you feel as this tree? . . .

What is your existence like? . . .

What do you experience?

Take some time to discover more about your life as this tree . . .

In a few moments I am going to ask you to get ready to return to your own existence in this room . . . Become aware of the floor under your feet . . . Feel the chair supporting your body . . . Become aware of your breathing and of the noises outside and the clock ticking here. When ready, open your eyes.'

(Eileen opens her eyes)

Now, Eileen, I would like you to express your experience of being that tree and I want you to do so in the first person, present tense. "I am a cherry blossom tree and I grow in a suburban garden. My roots stretch deep down through rich soil. My flowers are admired by people who pass by".

Therapist:	'And then as a tree . . .'
Eileen:	'Well . . .I was a great oak and I was growing inside a demesne wall and there were lots of other trees near me.'
Therapist:	'One second Eileen – I want you to stay in the present tense and be the tree – Could you begin "I am a great oak and I am growing inside a demesne wall and there are other trees near me".'
Eileen:	'Yes . . . I am growing near other trees and we are inside a demesne wall . . . I am a great oak tree, tall and sturdy. My long roots go down deep into the soil . . . I like being an oak tree . . . It is late autumn and my colourful leaves are like a rich carpet at my feet . . . and the little squirrels are collecting acorns . . . my leaves provide shelter for hedge-hogs . . . I feel proud that I am a source of food and shelter for these little creatures . . .'

(Silence).

Therapist:	'Anything else about you that you would like to describe?'
Eileen:	'Yes . . . there is a parcel, no not a parcel . . . it is more like a block . . . actually it is a stone . . . and it is suspended from one of the branches and I am wondering what it is doing there.'
Therapist:	'What do you feel right now?'
Eileen:	'I feel . . . this stone is not part of the tree . . . it is out of place and I wonder how it got on to the branch.'
Therapist:	'Can you be the tree and talk as it or as the branch, and tell me about this object hanging from you.'
Eileen:	'Well . . . it is grey . . . and heavy and uneven . . . it is a piece of limestone.'
Therapist:	'What shape is it?'
Eileen:	'It is uneven . . . bigger than a cup and it has jagged edges . . . not like the rounded stone by the seaside . . . just rough.'
Therapist:	'So a piece of rough, uneven limestone is hanging from one of your branches?'
Eileen:	'Yes . . . and I do not want it there.'
Therapist:	'I want you to imagine the stone can speak. What would it say?'
Eileen:	'Oh gosh! I do not know really.'
Therapist:	'What about starting it this way "I am a stone on the branch of an oak tree" . . .'
Eileen:	'I am a stone . . . and I am hanging on a branch . . . I am an unwanted load on this branch . . . and I am weighing it down . . .'

Therapist:	'Will you move to this other chair and be the branch and respond to the stone?' (Eileen switches chairs). 'You have just heard the stone say it is weighing you down. What do you say?'
Eileen:	(As branch). 'You are a nuisance . . . I was a happy tree but now you are a load on me. I do not want you here . . .'
Therapist:	'And the stone replies.' (Therapist signals to Eileen to move chairs.)
Eileen:	'It does not say anything . . . it is growing bigger and getting heavier.' (Eileen's hands were in a ball-shaped position, with the fingers on the right hand touching the fingers of the left hand. Then her thumbs and first three fingers opened out, making a wider shape with only the little fingers touching.)
Therapist:	'Are you aware of what your hands are doing?'
Eileen:	(Looking at her hands). 'They are in an open position as if . . .'
Therapist:	'As if . . .'
Eileen:	'They feel as if they are holding something . . . heavy.'
Therapist:	'The stone?'
Eileen:	'Yes . . . they feel like they are holding the stone.'
Therapist:	'Have you any notion what the stone is?'
Eileen:	'Well . . . yes . . . it has to do with something alright . . .'
Therapist:	'Do you know what the something is?'
Eileen:	'Yes . . . it is . . . about something I am worried about . . .'
Therapist:	'Uh-Uhah.'
Eileen:	'It is about a row . . . a misunderstanding, . . . with a friend . . . it is stupid really . . . but since it happened . . .'
Therapist:	'So your friend and yourself are not on good terms now and you feel upset about it?'
Eileen:	'Yes, I do.'
Therapist:	'What has happened?'
	(Eileen described the row between herself and her friend Maureen. She did dialogue work using the empty chair, got in touch with her hurt and eventually recognized the topdog/underdog conflict.)
Therapist:	Alright Eileen, your time is coming to an end and I know there is still unfinished business between Maureen and yourself, but I would like you to sum up what you feel right now and see if there is anything else you want to do before we stop.'
Eileen:	'Well, I know what that stone is and I am clearer about

where I stand with Maureen . . . and I realize I have been letting the row . . . weigh heavily on me . . . and I have decided not to let it dominate me.'

Therapist: 'Anything else Eileen?'

Eileen: 'I feel a sense of relief. I know I will need another session on it but I am clear on where to start. I do feel relief after that much.'

In working through this particular fantasy, various stages can be identified:

Stage one: the therapist sought first to ensure that the client was relaxed by paying attention to her body, breathing, thoughts and feelings.

Stage two: Eileen was invited to consider herself as a tree. Different aspects such as its bark, branches and surroundings were examined.

Stage three: the transition from the fantasy to interaction with the therapist was facilitated by asking the client to become aware of the floor, the chair, her breathing and the noises in the room.

Stage four: the therapist asked Eileen to recount her description of herself as a tree. When the client used the past tense, she was invited to change to the present tense.

Stage five: by describing herself as a tree, Eileen identified that there was a stone hanging from one of her branches. Its shape was then explored.

Stage six: a dialogue using the empty chair between the stone and the tree ensued. The therapist drew attention to the non-verbal behaviour of the client's hands, which led to the identification of a present conflict in Eileen's life, namely, a misunderstanding with a friend, Maureen.

Stage seven: Eileen described the conflict with Maureen. Her feelings of guilt and regret were explored. This caused Eileen to identify these feelings with the stone. She then spoke as the stone. A dialogue between Eileen and Maureen ensued, using the empty chair. This took the form of a topdog/underdog dialogue with Maureen as the topdog and Eileen as the underdog. By drawing attention to her use of qualifiers, the therapist enabled Eileen to realize that she did not regret what she had said. At this point Eileen indicated that she had come to the end of her work for the moment.

Stage eight: the therapist acknowledged that there is still unfinished business between Eileen and her friend. The session concluded with an invitation by the therapist to Eileen to sum up her feelings.

Chapter 7

Research investigations in gestalt therapy

INTRODUCTION

This chapter reviews reported studies in gestalt therapy. Very few research investigations had been undertaken before the late 1970s. In 1982, Simkin pointed out that most gestalt therapists were busy practising their technique rather than evaluating it: this is a defect common to most forms of counselling and psychotherapy. Practitioners frequently do not appreciate the value of research as it relates to their own professional life. The training of practitioners in research methodology is generally overlooked; on the other hand, the research of academics is often remote from experiences in the field. Thus there is a divergence between the priorities of academics and practitioners. In gestalt therapy, this gap has been accentuated, since training programmes are usually based in specialist gestalt institutes, rather than within research/university environments. What is needed is the use of a 'scientist practitioner' model in training, where trainee therapists receive a grounding in research as well as theory and practice. Without research, no substantiated claims can be made as to the effectiveness of gestalt therapy, or to the robustness of its methodology.

The benefits of gestalt therapy have been identified by Smith, Glass and Miller (1980). In a meta-analysis of 475 controlled studies of psychotherapy, an average 'effect size' was obtained for each of 18 therapy types (the effect size is the difference between the means of the experimental or treated group, and the untreated or control group on a given measure of change). This difference is divided by the standard deviation of the control group. Use of effect size has the advantage of not being dependent on the size of the sample as are statistical significance tests. Gestalt was, in general, as effective as other approaches, although fewer studies had been published in gestalt therapy. Smith *et al.* caution that the comparison is raw and uncontrolled, since people seeking psychological help do not randomly allocate themselves to the different types of therapy.

Meta-analysis allows the integration of a number of studies. Before such an analysis is possible, individual studies must, of course, be conducted.

The next session considers some studies which have been completed in the field.

RESEARCH IN GESTALT THERAPY

Research relating to gestalt therapy may be summarized under five headings:

1. Gestalt assumptions, process and goals;
2. Specific gestalt techniques;
3. Outcomes of gestalt groups;
4. The Gloria films;
5. Comparison with other approaches.

Gestalt assumptions, process and goals

Very few studies have been undertaken of gestalt assumptions, processes and goals. Raming and Frey (1974) applied content analysis and cluster analysis to the ideas of Fritz Perls, in order to develop a taxonomy of gestalt processes and goals. Important source material, namely *Gestalt therapy* (Perls, Hefferline and Goodman, 1951) and *Gestalt therapy verbatim* (Perls, 1969b) were selected as the inputs for content analysis. McQuilty's (1970) classification by multiple linkages generated three goal clusters and two process clusters. The goal clusters were the organism and the enviroment; self-awareness; and maturation and autonomy. The process clusters were skilful frustration of the client, and the here-and-now.

Summaries of these clusters were written. The goal cluster 'organism and environment' emphasized self-regulation, contact with the environment and the elements necessary for healthy communication. The 'self-awareness' goal cluster stressed that good contact is facilitated through awareness. Gestalt therapy brings experience into awareness. Internal processes are brought into the open while concentrating on bodily senses and movement. The 'maturation and autonomy' goal cluster identified three stages in the growth process, namely, (1) clients assimilate their reality, (2) actualize their potential, and (3) coordinate all that they are to be self-supportive. The process cluster 'skilful frustration of clients' indicates that the counsellor provides situations in which individuals experience what they want to avoid. Therapists help them to become aware of their avoidance and frustrate their attempts to resist the unpleasantness of the situation. This can take place at an internal or external level. The 'here-and-now' process cluster stresses the immediate context that the counsellor sets for the client's self-exploration.

As Raming and Frey (1974) point out, the study provides us with a paradigm that makes it possible to draft a short but accurate statement of Perls' work. It defines gestalt therapy as a process in which the counsellor seeks to skilfully frustrate the client in the here-and-now, so as to accentuate contact with the environment, self-awareness and maturation and autonomy.

Decreasing contact with the environment through neurotic verbalizations was the subject of a study by Nelson and Groman (1975). Neurotic verbalizations were classified into two major categories: avoidance of silence, and avoidance of responsibility. Avoidance of silence included filler phrases, echoing, inappropriate emphasizing, laughter and sighing. Avoidance of responsibility was manifested in qualifying statements, retractors and terminating statements. Gestalt therapy holds that the more neurotic individuals are, the more they will use avoidance in their speech.

On the basis of scores on the Neuroticism Scale of the Maudsley Personality Inventory (MPI), 106 college students were rank-ordered and divided into three groups – low, medium or high. Ten students were selected randomly from each of the three groups and assigned either to a neutral or to an emotionally charged condition. All subjects received a set of neutral questions. Depending on the treatment, they were then asked a further set of either neutral or emotionally charged questions. The verbal responses of the 30 subjects were recorded and analysed.

Emotionally charged questions led to more instances of neurotic verbalization. However, no significant relationship was found between neurotic verbalization and scores on the Maudsley Neuroticism Scale. The authors identify two possible reasons for this, namely, that the type of neurotic was not identified, obscuring possible differences in expression between hysterics and obsessive or dysthymic neurotics, and that neuroticism as defined by gestalt therapy and the MPI may not be identical. The MPI views neuroticism as a stable configuration of traits, while gestalt therapy views it as a situational response. Although the study does not support the gestalt assumption that the more neurotic individuals are, the more they will use avoidance in their speech, it does confirm that stressful questions result in a significantly greater number of neurotic verbalizations.

A further assumption of gestalt therapy is that neurotics avoid living in the present. Gestalt therapy views the use of past and future tenses as attempts to do this. In a follow-up study of 30 undergraduate volunteers, Nelson and Groman (1978) examined the relationship between temporal perspective and measures of neuroticism and anxiety. It was hypothesized that the more neurotic and/or anxious individuals would use more past and future tenses. As in the previous study, subjects were ranked low, medium or high on the Maudsley Neuroticism Scale. Each person was asked 18 questions, six each relating to past, present and future occurrences. For each group of six questions, three were emotionally negative or stressful and three were emotionally positive or non-stressful. Subjects were also asked to complete the Taylor Manifest Anxiety Scale and the State-Trait Anxiety Inventory.

All subjects used fewer present-tense verbs in ongoing stressful situations compared to neutral situations. However, highly neurotic individuals remained in the present to a greater extent than the medium or low neurotic groups. The authors again offer the stable trait versus situationist view of neuroticism as a possible explanation. In addition, they refer to a suggestion by Krauss *et al.* (1967) that images of past experiences and/or future expectations are capable of evoking various emotions in the present. They hypothesize that, for neurotic anxious individuals, the 'presentness' of the experimental situation can be viewed as a shelter which avoids either confronting the prospect of a seemingly unavoidable future, or dealing with unfinished business in the past.

The studies conducted by Nelson and Groman (1975, 1978) do not support either of the two gestalt assumptions investigated, namely that neurotic individuals will use avoidance in their speech and will avoid living in the present. However, it may be that the instrument used, the MPI, is not a valid measure in the context. Since Raming and Frey's (1974) study identifies the here-and-now as one of two valuable process clusters, an alternative measure to the MPI is required.

Specific gestalt techniques

The two-chair technique has been the subject of several investigations in the last decade: Greenberg and his co-workers (1979, 1980, 1981a, 1981b, 1982), Conoley *et al.* (1983), Clarke and Greenberg (1986) and Tyson and Range (1987). The first four studies compare the effectiveness of the two-chair technique with other methods, while the final four evaluate the two-chair experiment in the resolution of specific problems.

The differential effects of a gestalt two-chair experiment and *empathic reflection of feeling* by the therapist on (a) client depth of experiencing, (b) change in awareness, and (c) goal attainment, was studied by Greenberg and Clarke (1979). In an analogue study, 16 counselling psychology graduate students were selected from a pool of 21 volunteers and assigned to one of four counsellors.

The volunteers were asked to come to two experimental sessions to explore intrapersonal conflicts or splits. In the first session each counsellor used empathic reflection with two subjects, and a two-chair experiment in the second session. The order of presentation was reversed for the other two subjects. Both techniques sought to facilitate the resolution of personally meaningful conflicts. The measuring instruments completed by the subjects were the Focusing Questionnaire (Gendlin, 1968), the Experiencing Scale (Klien *et al*. 1969), the Goal Attainment Scale (Kiresuk and Sherman, 1968) the Personal Orientation Inventory (POI, Shostrom, 1966), a client report form of perceived change in awareness, and the Relationship Inventory (Barrett-Lennard, 1962).

Results showed that depth of experiencing and change in awareness were significantly higher for the subjects following the two-chair technique. There was no difference in the level of goal attainment following the two interventions. The study lends some support to the gestalt position that the two-chair technique leads to self-reported depth of experiencing and increased awareness.

In an analogue study on conflict resolution, Greenberg and Higgins (1980) compared the effects of the gestalt two-chair method with the effects of the **focusing technique followed by empathic reflection**. The subjects were 42 volunteers from a graduate counselling psychology programme. The Experiencing Scale, The Target Complaint Box Scale (Battle *et al.*, 1966), a change of awareness measure and a progress measure devised by the authors were administered. In addition, the students identified a felt intrapersonal conflict at the beginning of the interview. The students were randomly assigned to three groups of 14, one to engage in the gestalt two-chair intervention, another to experience focusing followed by empathic reflection, and the third to serve as a no-treatment control group. Volunteers in the first two groups were randomly assigned to one of seven counsellors for a session.

The two-chair dialogue produced significantly more depth of experiencing than did focusing plus empathic reflection. Greater change in awareness and progress in dealing with their issues occurred for both groups than for the no-treatment control. There was no difference in the amount of discomfort reduction between the three groups. Thus both studies identified an increase in depth of experiencing following the use of the two-chair technique.

Greenberg and Rice (1981) compared the effects of the gestalt two-chair experiment and **active empathy interventions** on client depth of experiencing and voice quality. The study involved three clients considered by therapists to be good-prognosis subjects for client-centred therapy. These clients were selected from 20 people interviewed at a university counselling centre. They compared the effects of three gestalt operations with three active empathy interventions on each client, with respect to conflict. Both sets of operation were applied under experimental control at similar points. The instruments used were Client Voice Quality (Rice and Wagstaff, 1967), the Focusing Questionnaire, the Experiencing Scale, and a client report form which sought subjective information on the perception of the session.

Results indicated that the gestalt two-chair operation led to a deepening of experiencing in the time period following the split for each of the three clients, whereas the active empathy operation did not. There was a substantial amount of focused voice quality for both gestalt and active empathy interventions. Greenberg and Rice interpreted the findings as suggesting that voice measures the subtle moment-by-moment process of involvement and focus, while depth of experiencing measures that process at a global level in terms of movement toward problem resolution. The clients' reports indicated that the gestalt sessions produced a more felt sense of change than the active empathy sessions. The investigators concluded that the main differences between the approaches appeared to be a function of the higher demand to directly experience and confront the split in the gestalt method. The size of the sample limits generalizations. Replication studies should be conducted with different therapists to ensure that the effects obtained were not due either to the particular therapists involved or to the therapist–client combinations used in this study.

In a similar experiment involving a larger sample of 10 counsellors and 16 clients, Greenberg and Dompierre (1981) also investigated the effects of the gestalt two-chair intervention and **empathic reflection of feeling** on client depth of experiencing and reported change in awareness. The counsellors worked at various urban counselling centres and in private practice, while the clients were those next on the waiting list. Each intervention was applied individually to help resolve conflicts expressed in counselling sessions. The measures used were the Relationship Inventory, the Target Complaint Box Scale and measures in change in awareness, conflict resolution, behaviour change and reported progress, which were created for the purposes of the project.

Results showed that depth of experiencing and shifts in awareness were higher following the gestalt intervention. The authors concluded that the gestalt two-chair dialogue appeared to encourage clients to actively confront and experience their conflict by making it alive and present. When empathic reflection was used, the client could talk about the conflict, but at a more cognitive level and with less of an immediate experience. Reported conflict resolution and behaviour change after the session and at a one-week follow-up was also greater for the gestalt approach. The level of discomfort after the session, however, was not significantly different for the two interventions.

In the same study, Greenberg and Dompierre (1981) found that trained counsellors' level of familiarity with the two-chair technique did not significantly influence its effectiveness. Six of the ten counsellors did not profess a gestalt orientation, but they had at least 50 hours of training in the use of the two-chair dialogue. The remaining four counsellors had at least 100 hours of training and 2–5 years of experience with the gestalt technique. The indications are that trained counsellors can learn to use this technique with little training. However, the effect of uncontrolled variables, such as level of intelligence and depth of counselling experience in other fields, need to be determined to verify the conclusion.

In a study of 31 clients, Greenberg and Webster (1982) conducted a 6-week programme using gestalt two-chair dialogue to work on intrapsychic conflict related to **decision-making**. The measuring instruments administered were the Client Vocal Quality System (Rice *et al.*, 1979), the Experiencing Scale and Benjamin's (1979) Structured Analysis of Social Behaviour. The clients were classified as resolvers or non-resolvers, based on a pattern of in-session process indicators.

Resolvers manifested three components in the process of conflict resolution: the voicing of criticism by one part of the personality; the expression of feelings and wants by another; and the softening in attitude of the 'critic'. Resolvers were found to be significantly less undecided and less anxious after treatment. They also reported greater improvement on target complaints and behaviour change. The study lends support to the topdog/underdog split outlined by Perls (1970).

A test of the foregoing three-stage sequential model of conflict resolution was conducted by Greenberg (1983). He compared 14 gestalt two-chair dialogue resolution performances with 14 non-resolution performances, to test the three-stage sequential model of conflict resolution previously outlined. Six therapists, trained in the gestalt approach, provided examples of resolution and non-resolution performances obtained from 28 clients. Measures used were the Structured Analysis of Social Behaviour, the Experiencing Scale, Client Vocal Quality System and client and therapist forms of the Conflict Resolution Box Scale.

In successful resolution of conflict, the two sides went through a stage of opposition and then entered a merging phase in which the critic softened its attitude, as measured by degree of affiliation, voice, and depth of experiencing. The mellowing of the attitude of the critic, indicated by softened voice, appeared to be a vital aspect. The degree of affiliation in the previously harsh critic in the dialogue clearly distinguished resolvers from non-resolvers. The study lends support to Polster and Polster's (1973) conclusion that 'the task in resolving the polarity is to aid each part to live to its fullest, while at the same time making contact with its polar counterpart' (p. 62). The results are limited to clients who engage in two-chair dialogue procedures. Replication studies need to be conducted in other environments, for example, cognitive–behavioural, to see if the components of the conflict resolution model proposed here still hold.

In an analogue study, Conoley *et al.* (1983) investigated the effect of (a) the empty-chair technique of gestalt therapy, (b) the ABCs of rational emotive therapy, and (c) a reflective listening control condition in reducing

anger for 61 female volunteer undergraduate students. The volunteers were randomly assigned to each of the three conditions. The Health and Opinion Questionnaire (Byrne, 1964), a portion of the MMPI which distinguishes between repressers and sensitizers, was used as an independent measure. The authors viewrepression–sensitization as an avoidance approach continuum. Repressers avoid stress, while sensitizers approach stress. Repressers deny anger and score higher on tests of emotional stabilty than do sensitizers. Because the empty-chair operation was hypothesized to highlight angry feelings, sensitizers should find it most effective in reducing their anger. The technique should capitalize on their predisposition to be in touch with emotions. On the other hand, it was predicted that the ABC use of cognitive control strategies would better suit the style of the repressers. Systolic blood pressure and a Feeling Questionnaire derived from Gough and Heilbrun's (1965) Adjective Checklist were used as dependent measures to assess anger level.

Both treatment techniques significantly reduced blood pressure and self-report levels of anger by clients. The represser–sensitizer measure failed to differentiate between the effectiveness of either treatment.

In a study in 1986, Clarke and Greenberg compared the gestalt two-chair intervention with a cognitive–behavioural problem-solving approach in resolving **decisional conflict**. Forty-eight clients were randomly assigned to three groups: a problem-solving group, a two-chair group, and a waiting-list control group. Counsellors saw clients for two sessions. Subjects were pre- and post-tested on Osipow, Carney and Barak's (1976) Scale of Vocational Indecision, and Harren's (1979) Assessment of Career Decision Making (ACDM), Part IV.

Results revealed that the gestalt two-chair intervention reduced indecision more effectively than did either cognitive–behavioural problem-solving or no treatment. Whereas previous investigations had concentrated on level of experiencing, focused voice quality and shifts in awareness, this study showed a significant effect on a direct measure of indecision. The investigators point out that although the study found changes on a self-report measure, it did not show evidence of decision implementation or concrete behavioural change. However, it is significant in that it showed the gestalt approach as being more effective than the cognitive–behavioural approach, i.e. gestalt clients reported being more decided than clients who tried to decide on a logical basis. It would appear that exploration of the feelings accompanying indecision is more fruitful than focusing on thoughts, with consequent changes in feelings. Behavioural measurements are required to concretize the results suggested in these studies.

The effect of empty-chair dialogue on **mild depression** was investigated by Tyson and Range (1987). Forty-four moderately depressed volunteer subjects were divided randomly into four treatment groups: attention-placebo, gestalt empty-chair dialogues designed to be personally relevant and high in affect, dialogues designed to be personally irrelevant and neutral in affect, and strong affect and no dialogues. Each group was led by the same person and met for 1 hour per week for 4 weeks. All subjects were pretested, post-tested, and a follow-up was carried out using an abbreviated form of the MPI, the Depression Adjective Checklist, and experimenter-devised questionnaires.

The results indicated that mild depression, as well as anxiety and social introversion, dissipated over a month and remained lower regardless of whether the subject had any treatment. Furthermore, these benefits were still present 2 months later. The empty-chair dialogue did not prove to be significantly better than other methods in working with mild depression. Since the same counsellor was used in all four conditions, he/she appears to have been equally effective in each case. This finding could be an artefact of the personality of the counsellor.

The research studies outlined in this section support the effectiveness of the gestalt two-chair technique. Its use led to greater depth of experiencing and increased awareness on the part of the client than did empathic reflection as a method of producing change of felt conflict. This sense of conflict resolution persisted over a week. Clients also reported significantly more change in target behaviours. The two-chair technique emerged as a very useful intervention in handling conflict problems. It was clear that trained counsellors may use it after as little as 50 hours of training.

OUTCOMES OF GESTALT GROUPS

During the 1970s a series of studies was conducted by Foulds and his co-authors on the outcomes of gestalt groups. Since then Côté (1982), Swain (1989) and O'Leary and Page (1990) have investigated this area.

Guinan and Foulds (1970) conducted a 30-hour weekend marathon group with 10 volunteer college students using an experiential gestalt orientation. An equal number of students volunteered for a non-treatment group which was controlled for sex, age and college class. The Personal Orientation Inventory (POI) (Shostrom, 1965, 1966) was used as an index of change or personal growth. Pretest and post-test results indicated significant changes in a positive direction in the mean scores of the marathon group participants on the following scales: inner direction, existentiality, feeling reactivity, spontaneity, self-acceptance, acceptance of aggression, capacity for intimate contact. There were no significant changes for the non-treatment group.

However, the study suffers from certain weaknesses. At the pretest stage, significant differences were found between the mean scores of the two groups. The use of separate self-selection procedures for both the marathon and the non-treatment control group may have contributed to this difference. It is possible that college students who volunteer for gestalt marathon workshops may not be representative of college students in general.

The design of Guinan and Foulds' (1970) study was improved in a further investigation of a 24-hour marathon gestalt group by Foulds and Hannigan (1976a). Thirty-six volunteer college students were randomly assigned by sex to experimental and control groups each containing nine males and nine females. On this occasion, no significant differences were found between pretest mean scores of the two groups on the POI scale.

Findings revealed a significant positive pre–post change in the marathon group's overall level of self-actualization, and on 11 of 12 POI subscales. No significant changes occurred for the control group on any of the measures. A 6-month follow-up of the marathon group was conducted, which indicated a significant change in the overall level of self-actualization, and in seven of the 12 POI subscales. Since the control group was not followed up at 6 months, no conclusions can be drawn as to the significance of these effects.

An almost identical replication study was conducted by the authors in the same year (1976b). On this occasion, larger numbers of volunteers were randomly assigned to both groups, giving 36 participants in the 24-hour gestalt marathon workshop and 36 non-treatment control students. The findings of this replication study were highly similar to the original one. Significant positive changes in the self-actualization of volunteer college students on the POI were observed following a 24-hour gestalt marathon workshop. Since no test of the non-treatment control group occurred at the 6-month follow-up, no conclusions can be drawn.

The POI was again used to measure self-actualization of volunteer college students in a study by Foulds and Hannigan (1977). A Solomon four-group design was employed to study the effects of a 32-hour gestalt workshop. Sixty subjects were randomly assigned by sex to four subgroups. Analysis of variance indicated positive changes on overall self-actualization and on ten of the 12 subscales of the POI. No significant pretest sensitization effects or interaction effects were observed on any of the POI scales; the observed changes thus appear to be the result of the gestalt workshop and suggest that it may be an effective method for fostering the personal growth of college students.

A gestalt marathon workshop was also investigated by Foulds and Hannigan (1976c), but on this occasion they administered the Eysenck Personality Inventory (EPI). Eighteen volunteer college students were subjects for the 24-hour workshop, while a further 18 served as a non-treatment control. The workshop promoted emotional stability and reduced neurotic blocks to the psychological development of the students, although there were no changes on the measure of extroversion–introversion. The continued existence of this effect was not established since no follow-up measures were used.

A final study on the effects of a 24-hour marathon workshop was conducted by the same authors in 1978. Thirty-six undergraduate volunteers were randomly assigned to either the gestalt group or to the non-treatment control. The group led to positive changes in the self-description of participants on those scales of the California Personality Inventory (CPI) which deal with intrapsychic functioning. More specifically, it enabled greater change in personal functioning than in social functioning. A weakness of the study lies in the lack of any follow-up testing.

The contribution of an intensive gestalt therapy group in reaching the developmental goals of enrichment of personality was the subject of an investigation by Côté (1982). Sixty people, divided into three groups of 20, participated in the study. In addition, they selected a partner from among their close relatives who reported on observed changes during the experience. One group underwent 5 days of intensive gestalt group therapy. A second group visited Haiti, where they took part in a number of activities aimed at stimulating their awareness of the local way of living, while a control group pursued their regular activities at home and at work. Changes were measured by two tests, the Personal Orientation Inventory (Shostrom, 1966) and the TERCI, a Quebec adaptation of the Interpersonal Check List of LaForge and Suczek (1955). Three open-ended questionnaires examined possible reasons for changes in self-perceptions. In addition, partners of participants were asked for changes they might have noticed during the experience, and for descriptions of participants on the TERCI.

Results indicated that the gestalt group had contributed to the enhancement of self-actualization of the participants, and that progress made by subjects was maintained 4 months later. The perception of positive changes by participants was verified by both the POI results and the evaluations of partners. The group which travelled did not change significantly in comparison to the control group: no modification occurred in the personality of these participants. The study does not determine what aspects of gestalt therapy are most likely to foster the development of the individual.

The shortest gestalt group reported in the literature is that in a study by Swain (1989). Sixteen volunteer undergraduate college students were randomly allocated to either a gestalt group which lasted for 7 hours, or to a non-treatment control. The measures used were the Rosenberg (1965) Self-esteem Scale and a sociometric form devised by the author which measured group cohesiveness. Pre-, post- and 6-week follow-up tests were administered to both groups.

Statistical analyses of change scores revealed no differences in self-esteem between the treatment and non-treatment control group members. Cohesiveness was significantly greater for the treatment group participants at post-test and follow-up. The generalizability of the findings is limited by the small sample size and the volunteer nature of the participants.

In a study of a 20-hour person-centred gestalt group, O'Leary and Page (1990) assessed the types of attitude changes that occurred. Both experimental and control groups consisted of four female and three male college students. Subjects were measured on the evaluative and potency scales of the semantic differential concepts of awareness, responsibility, gestalt therapy, anger, my real self, my ideal self, fear, love, guilt, past, future and self-acceptance. A quasi-experimental pretest/post-test controlled group design was used.

Results indicated that the members of the experimental group increased their scores significantly more than the non-treatment group participants on the potency scales of the concepts of future, love and gestalt therapy. No differences were discovered for the evaluative scales. This finding illustrates the purpose of gestalt groups, and deals with emotions rather than values. Participants viewed the group as a positive experience since they had stronger feelings about gestalt therapy. Because relationships with significant others were discussed in the group, the authors felt that stronger feelings about love were not unexpected. Since the future was not a major topic in the group, a significant increase in feelings about the future was surprising. The authors suggested that by spending a considerable amount of time dealing with unfinished business in the past, participants had stronger feelings about the future. As individuals let go of past concerns they were increasingly aware of future events.

These studies indicate that gestalt groups can increase the self-actualization of college students. Further follow-up studies are needed to see if this effect persists over time.

The POI was the most frequently used instrument in the outcome studies reported in this section. Significant changes on subscales as a result of treatment were not reported, apart from the Guinan and Foulds' (1970) study. This decision was based on Bloxom's (1985) statement that the subscales have at least five items in common with each other, and are therefore not statistically independent. However, its two major scales, time competence and inner support, are free of this problem if used by themselves. Hence it would seem appropriate to retain the POI for research purposes, given the significance of inner support for gestalt therapy. Inner support is defined in the POI as the tendency of a person to act on and be guided by his/her own principles and motives, in contrast to responding to a wide variety of external pressures. Coan (1985) notes that Shostrom used the thinking of Perls in developing his items. This thinking is apparent in the POI in its use of inner support as one of the basic characteristics of the self-actualizer.

The use of tests such as the POI to assess personal growth and change through gestalt therapy places an obligation on the researcher to examine other psychometric properties of the scores obtained. The Rust Statement (1989) draws attention to the need to evaluate the reliability of differences between scores as a measure of change.

Test scores, however, are but one means of measuring change in outcome studies. In Côté's (1982) investigation, an observation of change by partners was also obtained. Multiple measures are desirable which consider not only self-reported change by the client, but behavioural change as observed by a third party.

The Gloria film

The Gloria film, *Three approaches to psychotherapy*, is included in this section because it is the accepted demonstration of Perls' technique. In this film, Carl Rogers, Fritz Perls and Albert Ellis counselled the same client, Gloria. A content analysis study was carried out by Zimmer and Cowles (1972). Selected words and co-occurrences of words within sentences were used as dependent variables. Frequencies and ratios were generated for analysis. Contradictory findings were obtained. The use of frequency measures found that a client behaved differently with different therapists, whereas the use of ratio measures led to the opposite conclusion. Since the more direct measure is frequency not ratio, it can be concluded that the client did behave differently with different therapists.

Meara, Shannon and Pepinsky (1979) used data generated from a computer-assisted language analysis system, and excerpts taken from two different time periods in each interview from the Gloria film. They compared the stylistic complexity of the language of counsellors and clients in different approaches to therapy: client-centred (Rogers), rational–emotive (Ellis) and gestalt (Perls). The assumption underlying the study was that unless client and counsellor can signal to each other their interpretations of what is taking place, and reach a common understanding, no progress in counselling can occur. Four dependent measures of stylistic complexity were used: (1) number of sentences, (2) average sentence length, (3) average block length, and (4) average clause depth.

Results indicated that the counsellors were significantly different from one another on each of the four measures. Rogers had the lowest number of sentences with 18, Ellis the highest with 47, and Perls uttered almost as many sentences as Ellis (40) and significantly more than Rogers. The average sentence length was greatest for Ellis, with 4.2 clauses per sentence, least for Perls with 2.2, with Rogers in between at 3.1. Perls' high sentence output indicated that he was active, whereas his low average sentence length reflected the confrontational nature of his interventions. From his high number of sentences and average sentence length, Ellis showed that he was an active explainer who used frequent, detailed, elaborate and complex sentences. The low number of sentences used by Rogers confirmed his infrequent responses. His average sentence length, however, was longer than Perls', indicating that he was not as brief and stylistically simple as the investigators had anticipated.

The average block length and average clause depth yielded similar results. Ellis required the client to process more complex information, speaking at the rate of 157 subordinate clauses for every 100 main clauses. This contrasted with Rogers' pattern of 106 subordinate clauses for every 100 main clauses, and Perls' very simple style of 72 subordinate clauses for every 100 main clauses. This pattern was maintained for average clause depth.

As for Gloria, she spoke least with Ellis (24 sentences), most with Perls (60 sentences) and at an intermediate rate with Rogers (44 sentences). The average sentence length was greatest with Rogers and least with Perls. In terms of average block length and average clause depth, Gloria's interaction with Rogers was less complex than with Ellis. This indicates that a common understanding had been established between Gloria and both Perls and Rogers. However, a factor ignored in this study was the amount of time each counsellor devoted to the client.

This factor was taken into account by Kiesler and Goldston (1988). They noted that the interaction with Gloria lasted 30 minutes for Rogers, 20 minutes for Perls, and 15 minutes for Ellis. On this basis, they controlled for duration by taking only the first 15 minutes of each interaction. Seventy-two undergraduate psychology students viewed and rated either Gloria or the therapist on the Check List of Psychotherapy Transactions.

Significant differences emerged in the interpersonal behaviour of (a) the three therapists with Gloria, and (b) Gloria with the three. Rogers was significantly friendlier and less dominant than Perls with Gloria. Gloria was clearly more amicable with both Rogers and Ellis than with Perls. On the other hand, she was significantly more dominant with Perls than with either Rogers or Ellis.

The study offers the first analysis of interpersonal behaviours in the Gloria film. It casts doubt on the previously held belief that Rogers' approach leads to the empowerment of the client, since Gloria was more dominant with Perls. Kiesler and Goldston (1988) present a note of caution, however, with regard to the findings. Since judgements by raters were made 15 minutes after viewing a film, this can add unknown amounts of selective attention and recall that are theoretically considered to be related to the preferred interpersonal styles of the raters themselves. Whereas it is obviously desirable to control the time factor in some manner, the way in which it is done in this study (by simply truncating the Rogers and Perls interviews) is very questionable, since it very seriously undermines the integrity of each of these interviews.

In a study by Hill, Thames and Rardin (1979), transcripts of the Gloria film were analysed by three judges using the Hill Counsellor Verbal Response Category System. A verbal response unit was defined by the authors as an independent clause consisting minimally of a subject, object and verb. Each of the three sessions was divided into three temporal units, so that variations within and between counsellors over time could be studied.

Behavioural differences between the three approaches were discovered. The therapists showed differing patterns in responses: across the entire session Perls used direct guidance (19%), information (12%), interpretation (12%), open question (10%), minimal encouragers (8%), closed question (6%), confrontation (6%), approval–reassurance (5%) and non-verbal referent (5%). Minimal encouragers were established as the principal response mode of Rogers, since he employed them 53% of the time. He also engaged in restatement (11%), interpretation (7%), reflection (7%), and information (7%). The information response was most characteristic of Ellis (3%), while other responses were direct guidance (21%), minimal encouragers (14%), interpretation (12%), closed questions (6%) and re-statement (5%).

An interesting difference in the dynamic of the interview is seen between the three counsellors. Across the three parts of the interview, Perls decreased his use of closed questions, open questions and non-verbal referents. More frequent use of approval–reassurance, direct guidance and self-disclosure is evident in the middle third, compared to the beginning and end. Roger engaged in fewer minimal encouragers and less information, and a greater number of restatements in the middle third, compared with the beginning and end. Ellis showed a consistent decrease in the number of minimal encouragers, restatements and interpretations, and a consistent increase in information and direct guidance.

Perls was the only therapist to use confrontation and non-verbal refe-rents (11%) indicating that gestalt therapy focuses on these two areas. Hill, Thames and Rardin (1979) concluded that Perls' repertoire of responses was wider than either Rogers' or Ellis' and that he did not rely on any one type. However, a cautionary note is appropriate with respect to these findings: the authors discovered that restatement, reflection, interpretation and confrontation appeared to be highly related and difficult to differentiate in the Hill Counsellor Verbal Response Category System. Since the construct validity of this instrument is questionable, no conclusions can be made with respect to its findings.

Mercier and Johnson (1984) investigated the Gloria film with particular reference to predicate use in the counsellor and client representational system. Representational systems, according to Bandler and Grinder (1975, 1979), are conceptual maps which people use to build internal models of the world, to process information and to guide behaviour. The representational system may be either visual, auditory or kinaesthetic. The basic scoring unit was the predicate, i.e. verbs, adverbs and adjectives. These predicates were then classified by representational system and totalled. Two judges, unfamiliar with the techniques of Bandler and Grinder, were trained on both predicate identification and representational system classification, until they reached agreement levels of 75%.

Results revealed that the primary representational system of both Gloria and Rogers was kinaesthetic. Rogers used more kinaesthetic predicates than Perls, but Perls' use of them increased over the course of the session. Ellis' primary representational system was auditory. Mercier and Johnson (1984) point out that this 'does fit with the cognitive model's view that people's responses are influenced by the things they "tell themselves"' (p. 167).

Sequential analyses revealed that the behaviour of both Perls and Rogers towards Gloria was characterized by accommodation to each other's speech. This was manifested in Rogers and Gloria's efforts to stabilize their use of kinaesthetic predicates. However, Perls and Gloria also appeared to reach a consensus on the use of the kinaesthetic mode as their joint primary representational system. No such agreement occurred between Ellis and Gloria. Ellis used the auditory system throughout, while Gloria varied her use of method with him. The study provides support for the two-way nature of counselling in the case of Perls and Rogers.

In summary, the picture of Perls which emerges from these studies is that of an active, confrontational therapist who uses a wide repertoire of responses and pays particular attention to Gloria's non-verbal behaviour. Perls' approach led to more client self-empowerment. His primary representational system was kinaesthetic, and his accommodation to Gloria's representational system reflects the two way nature of counselling.

The attempt to compare the performance of the counsellors in the above studies has an inherent weakness in that it presupposes that the attitude of the client is unchanged from one interview to another. In addition, there was no control for the effect of the order in which the counsellors interviewed the client. The Gloria film is of some use in describing the three counselling approaches as presented by their chief exponents, but of dubious value in comparing their effectiveness.

COMPARISON WITH OTHER APPROACHES

There are five relevant studies which fall into this category. In 1978, Anderson compared the effects of gestalt sensory awareness – *Rogerian encounter and self-directed encounter groups* – on intermember empathy, cohesiveness and feelings of alienation. Volunteers were randomly assigned to one of eight groups, with 10 subjects in each. There were six treatment groups and two control groups. Two treatment groups were assigned to each of the three approaches. Four of the groups (three treatment and one control) were both pre- and post-tested and four (three treatment and one control) received only post-tests. The six treatment groups met once a week for 3 hours for 4 consecutive weeks. The measures used were the Keniston Alienation Scale, Gordon's Sense of Self-Autonomy Scale, the Interpersonal Perception Method of Laing, Phillipson and Lee (1966) and the Feelings about the Group Instrument of Lieberman, Yalom and Miles (1973).

All treatment groups experienced significantly decreased feelings of alienation and an increased sense of self-autonomy. The order of efficacy on outcomes was (1) self-directed encounter, (2) Rogerian encounter and (3) gestalt sensory awareness. Increases in intermember empathy, feelings of being understood by other group members, and cohesiveness, were found in the same order. A possible limitation of the gestalt sensory-awareness group was that it was operationalized by the prescriptive programme developed by Stevens (1971). This was based on Perls' gestalt therapy theory. A series of leader-initiated experiments was presented to members. The methodology was more akin to individual therapy in the group, as practised by Perls. Given that some of the outcomes being tested were intermember empathy, feelings of being understood by group members, and cohesiveness, a more appropriate method might have been the floating hotseat, as outlined by Polster and Polster (1973), which includes the spontaneous participation of the rest of the group.

A further limitation of the study lay in the nature of the self-directed encounter group experience. This approach, based on Berzon and Reisel (1976), borrowed heavily from the other two approaches used in the study. It stressed the member interaction of the Rogerian encounter group and the here-and-now experience of the gestalt sensory awareness exercises. Given these limitations, a study similar to that undertaken by Raming and Frey (1974) (already outlined above) needs to be carried out to identify the goal and process clusters of these self-directed encounter groups. This would identify the extent of the overlap in treatments between the three groups investigated by Anderson (1978).

Preferences for gestalt, **behavioural and analytic psychotherapy** were investigated by Sobel (1979). Forty females and 27 males from middle-class or working-class backgrounds, were selected from the first-year classes of two state colleges in the USA. All participants were unmarried, their average age was 18.6 years. A further 40 females with an average age of 45.9 years, who fell into class III or class IV of the Hollingshead Two factor index of social position, were chosen from an adult evening school. None of the subjects had had previous psychotherapy experience. The author designed audio-recordings of analytic, behavioural and gestalt therapy, focusing on salient aspects of the particular therapy, deleting evaluative comments and avoiding identification of both the method and technical language used. High interjudge reliability and agreement were obtained.

Young females were the only group with a significant preference for therapy type, namely gestalt. In dealing with phobias, both young and old females, but not young males, significantly preferred behavioural therapy. As a combined group, young males and young females clearly chose the therapist–client relationship in both gestalt and analytic therapy. Under forced-choice conditions, the total group preferred gestalt therapy. However, no indications was given as to the reasons for their choice.

In a study of the verbal therapeutic behaviour of gestalt, **psychoanalytic-oriented and behaviour** therapists, Brunink and Schroeder (1970) invited six people from each of the three approaches to submit a taped therapy session beyond the third interview. Therapist behaviour was measured by a content analysis. Results indicated that therapists from all three groups were similar in their communication of empathy. Compared to the other two groups, gestalt therapists provided more direct guidance, more self-disclosure, greater initiative, less verbal facilitation, less focus on the clients and less emotional support. The study lends support to the popular perception of gestalt therapy as an active, directive style of interaction.

A comparison of therapist orientation and theoretical attitudes toward therapy was conducted by Peterson and Bradley (1980). Fifty-four therapists, 17 gestalt, 17 **behavioural** and 20 **rational emotive (RET)**, participated in the study. All were members of institutes or organizations in their particular specialty, while self-report verification of theoretical orientation was also obtained.

Attitudinal differences between the three groups seemed primarily to reflect variations in theoretical orientation; gestalt therapists scored highest on the affect subscale, behavioural therapists on the behavioural subscale and RET therapists on the cognitive subscale. Differences in attitudes toward client-centred therapy emerged; gestalt therapists recognized the importance of developing a safe, trusting counselling atmosphere through the characteristics of congruence, authenticity, warmth and unconditional positive regard. This indicated a belief in the dialogical approach to gestalt therapy, as propounded by Polster and Polster in Hycner (1987). Both behavioural and RET counsellors held ambivalent attitudes towards this viewpoint.

In a study of therapists of gestalt, **psychoanalytic and behavioural** orientations, verbatim transcripts were content-analysed by Bouchard *et al.* (1987) using the Therapist Inferential Communication System (TICS), which differentiates between inferential and non-inferential categories. Inferential categories are direct or indirect opinions which increase client self-exploration or self-understanding, and convey a meaning beyond the immediately available evidence. The non-inferential category includes passive acceptances, minimal encouragers and silences, and therapeutic interventions such as modelling, systematic desensitization and role playing. Therapeutic interventions comprise concrete actions on the therapists' part which communicate no additional inferential meaning. Inferential power is hypothesized to decrease across six categories: direct opinion, evaluative judgement, verbal or non-verbal referent, awareness, selective attending, and information seeking.

Gestalt therapists spent half of the time working with awareness. Behavioural therapists worked significantly less on awareness than the other two groups combined, and showed more interest in immediate experience more frequently than the other two groups combined. Psychodynamic therapists used more frequent direct opinions and invitations to explore than did the other two groups combined. The study confirmed that theoretical orientation influenced the use of inferential communications. It also supported the preeminence of awareness in gestalt therapy.

The studies outlined above found that gestalt therapy was an active approach. It involved more direct guidance, more self-disclosure, greater initiative and less verbal facilitation than either behavioural or psychodynamic approaches. Although there was less emotional support for, and less focus on, the client in gestalt, the therapists valued a safe, trusting counselling atmosphere. There was a general preference among clients for gestalt therapy over the other two therapies. Support for the orientation and theoretical attitudes of gestalt therapists was evident, and their emphasis on the use of awareness was confirmed.

Chapter 8

Methods, issues and new directions in gestalt therapy

INTRODUCTION

In this chapter, methods used in research in gestalt therapy are described. Problems arising from the research reported in Chapter 7 are examined, and new directions in gestalt therapy are outlined.

RESEARCH METHODS IN GESTALT THERAPY

At the outset it needs to be stated that there is no unique, optimal way for conducting research; rather it depends on the phenomenon which is being investigated. The two main methods used to date in gestalt therapy research have been the experimental analogue and the therapeutic situation itself, focused on either the individual or the group. The experimental analogue has a relatively narrow and concentrated frame of reference, which allows for specificity of factors and makes it an excellent tool for examining causal relationships. The therapist engages in specific counsellor behaviours and the effects on the client are measured. In investigations of the therapeutic situation involving one-to-one or group gestalt therapy, the emphasis is on the therapeutic process as it occurs, or on outcomes that emerge. The relevance of these studies is enhanced by this approach, which, however, diminishes its preciseness.

With analogue studies in particular, the subjects are often students or adult volunteers. The crucial issue is the generalizability of the results to client populations. Two possibilities emerge: the use of client samples in experimental analogue studies, or replication studies with actual clients. Replication studies determine the reliability and generalizability of research results. Reliability means results are consistent. In systematic replication studies the questions under consideration remain the same, but the type of subject and the environment, for example, group or individual, are systematically altered one at a time.

Given that gestalt therapy is practised in either group or one-to-one settings, a range of methodologies needs to be considered. In group therapy, one of three designs referred to by Campbell and Stanley (1963) as 'true experimental designs' (p. 13) may be employed. These are the pretest post-test, control group design; Solomon's four-group design; and the post-test only, control group design. Solomon's four-group design uses a treatment group and a control group in addition to the pretest, post-test, control group design. Neither of these two extra groups are pretested, thus allowing the separation of the main effects of testing and the interaction of testing and treatment. In addition, multiple analyses of the treatment effects is obtained. The post-test only, control group design uses randomization of subjects to the treatment and control groups. This design is based on the fact that the most effective method of ensuring lack of difference at the baseline between treatment and control groups on the variables being measured, is randomization. Consequently, the use of a pretest is not considered necessary.

Although these three experimental designs satisfy the demands of the scientific method, field factors such as life events often operate for the gestalt therapist, which diminishes the possibilities for experimental manipulation and adequate control. The use of quasi-experimental approaches in such instances would seem preferable to the absence of any endeavour to discover what is occurring. They do not, however, meet the full requirements of experimental control, and hence caution must be exercised in recognizing the limits of the results obtained. One inherent difficulty is that individuals can rarely be assigned randomly to treatment groups. The non-randomization of subjects remains the distinguishing feature in many pretest post-test quasi-experimental design. Although the random selection of participants does not occur, both experimental and control groups can be matched on relevant characteristics. Yet the use of a group design which does not include randomization reduces the predictive power of the conclusions.

The use of the case study in one-to-one gestalt therapy would appear to be particularly appropriate. Measurable responses from a single subject, obtained under controlled conditions, are presented in detail. A controlled independent variable, such as counsellor behaviour, is introduced and its effects on the client's responses are observed; the use of videotapes has resulted in much greater precision in this area. Since therapists are subject to their own within-rater variability, videotapes allow evaluation by different raters. Case studies are particularly appropriate when the research is in a relatively unexplored area, as they can result in the formulation of hypotheses which can be experimentally tested. Generalizations from case studies, however, can only be accepted if their validity is confirmed by more objective means.

Yin *et al.* (Yin and Heald, 1975; Yin, Bingham and Heald, 1976) offer a case-survey method for quantifying case studies. Each study is rated on several dimensions, such as research quality, programme characteristics and outcomes. These multiple ratings are then accumulated across studies, giving an overall numerical summary. Since such summaries are not rigorously quantitative, they cannot be compared directly with effect sizes or significance levels. Nevertheless they do provide a rough estimate of the cumulative effect of treatment in one therapeutic setting.

The use of questionnaires and tests in gestalt therapy assumes that they reliably and validly assess the constructs in question. It is desirable to possess quantitative and qualitative information concerning the scales. Along with a numeric estimate of reliability, information on construct validity is necessary. Thus one knows conceptually what the scale measures.

Construct validity is of particular importance, since constructs are hypothetical abstractions for which there is no single agreed-upon operational index. Constructs, however, are always related, directly or indirectly, to behaviour or experience. Not surprisingly, the better-defined the construct is, the easier it is to determine construct validity. Detailed descriptions of the relationship between the construct and a number of different behaviours can assist in the establishment of construct validity. Thus the construct 'anger' suggests that a number of non-verbal behaviours may be associated with it, such as clenching the fist or tightening the jaw. Measures of these non-verbal behaviours should be positively correlated with measures of anger.

The standard approach to evaluating construct validity involves the examination of convergent and discriminant validity coefficients (Davis, 1987). A measure with construct validity should correlate highly with measures of related constructs, or with different measures purporting to assess the same construct. For example, the correlations between a test measuring anger, observers' ratings of anger, and friends' ratings of anger, indicate whether these three methods are related to each other. On the other hand, a measure should have a low correlation with measures of unrelated constructs.

Construct validity may also be established by means of factor analysis. The description of a construct provides information about the expected relationships between variables; factor analysis confirms whether these relationships in fact exist. Experimental manipulation of the construct can also provide measures of construct validity. In the measurement of anger, for example, a test should show higher scores for subjects who are placed in a frustrating situation than for subjects who are not.

Within therapy there has been a tendency to use self-report measures. According to Millham and Jacobsen (1978), self-report measures suffer from a set of contaminants such as memory distortion, selective perception, subject acquiescence and social desirability. Non-self-report measures, for example behaviour observation scales, have not been subjected to the same scrutiny. Howard (1982) stated that the generalizability of non-self-report measures can be limited by such factors as method variance, situation variance, behavioural unreliability, rater variance and obtrusive measurement variance. Thus it would seem desirable to use a combination of self-report and behavioural measures in any research study of gestalt therapy. The next section examines emerging research issues in gestalt therapy.

EMERGING RESEARCH ISSUES IN GESTALT THERAPY

To date, the two-chair technique (Greenberg and associates) and group outcomes (Foulds and associates) are the only areas in gestalt therapy that have been subjected to systematic investigation. Gurman and Razim (1977) point out that 'science builds not on the single study, but on sets of studies with similar findings' (p. 24). Given the small sample size in most of the research of Greenberg *et al.* and Foulds *et al.*, for example, further replication studies are needed on gestalt techniques and group outcomes. Replication studies are also needed which consider gestalt assumptions, process and goals.

The studies reported in Chapter 7 vary with respect to the amount of information provided on the reliability and validity of scales. Many of them (e.g. Foulds and Hannigan, 1976, 1977; Greenberg and Clarke, 1979; Greenberg and Higgins, 1980; Greenberg and Rice, 1981; Tyson and Range, 1987; Swain, 1989) provide one or more citations where such information may be obtained. Others offer more detail; for example, O'Leary and Page (1990) provide quantitative information on reliability and citations for validity. A content validation procedure is described by Peterson and Bradley (1980). Similar information is given by Bouchard *et al.* (1987) along with quantitative information on reliability. None of these studies report convergent and discriminant validity coefficients. Little progress can be made in gestalt therapy research until studies are based on reliable and valid measures. Theory-building and inferences as a result of research is thus hindered. It is desirable that future studies should contain a quantitative measure of reliability. Furthermore, Meir and Davies (1980) suggest that researchers ought to provide a correlation with the best competing convergent scale, along with a correlation of a scale that clearly measures a distinct construct. If such data are unavailable from reported literature, they could be gathered as part of pilot testing.

A variety of designs were employed in the outcome studies outlined in Chapter 7. Foulds and Hannigan (1976a, b) and Swain (1989) used a pretest post-test control design: this is the most frequently used design in outcome studies of gestalt therapy. A Solomon four-group design was used by Foulds and Hannigan (1977) which allowed the treatment effect to be determined in four different ways. A quasi-experimental pretest post-test design with self-selection by subjects into either the experimental or the control group was also employed (Guinan and Foulds, 1970).

Two main issues emerge from the previous discussion. Firstly, where self-selection into treatment and control groups occurs, uncontrolled elements will influence the results: subject differences rather than treatment differences may account for the obtained effects. In the Guinan and Foulds (1970) study the self-selection of students into the treatment group may have meant that only those individuals who felt gestalt therapy would be beneficial chose to participate in this group. The outcome of the treatment, then, may have been a function of both self-selection into treatment and control groups and the treatment itself. Randomization of subjects into these groups overcomes this difficulty, and should be used in all outcome studies. The control group can then provide a baseline in order to determine the effects of the treatment.

The second issue which emerges relates to sampling. In general, the larger the sample size, the greater the degree of possible extrapolation of the findings to the population under consideration. However, the representativeness of a sample is more important than size. The essential condition for this is the selection of subjects in a random manner. Of the studies reported in Chapter 7, a large number (Foulds and Hannigan, 1976; Anderson 1978; Greenberg and Higgins, 1980; Guinan and Foulds, 1970; Swain, 1989) came from narrowly defined subpopulations such as volunteer subjects in a particular year and programme. It is desirable that future samples from student populations be obtained from the total student population in a particular year and programme. Such an approach is preferable to the present practice of concentrating solely on volunteers, which severely limits the generalization of the findings.

Given the importance of outcome studies in establishing the effectiveness of gestalt therapy, it is surprising that few studies have dealt with this topic. Inherent outcome measurement difficulties may be largely responsible.

Outcome is not a single variable but encompasses (1) the professional report of the therapist, (2) reports by observers who are close to clients while in their homes, at work or at leisure, and (3) the self-reports of clients. Outcome studies need to include these differing measures. In addition, outcome measurement is optimal when follow-up studies are conducted using varying time intervals such as 2 weeks, 4 weeks, 6 months, 1 year and 3 years. It is too easy to succumb to a 1-week or 2-week time interval on the pretext of difficulty of contacting group members once the group has disbanded. One solution to this involves a contract made with the participants at the outset, concerning a follow-up investigation. Adequate planning is a critical aspect of well designed follow-up studies.

Studies of process and investigations of outcome have tended to be conducted separately. Investigations which relate successful in-therapy performances to observed changes outside therapy are needed. In order to achieve this, three types of outcome – immediate, intermediate and final – and three levels of process – speech act, episode and relationship – need to be examined, as Greenberg (1986) points out. Immediate outcome refers to the change evident in the session that results from a specific intervention or from the final interaction. Observations by judges of videotapes of both therapists' and clients' behaviours could offer behavioural measures in this area. Gurman and Razim (1977) suggest that these two sets of judgements should be made by two separate groups of judges, and the results corre-lated over therapy hours. Intermediate outcomes would include change outside sessions in behaviours and attitudes, while final outcomes are those apparent at the end of treatment and at follow-up.

Speech acts are what one person says or does to another. Paralinguistic variables are included in this category. Perls' (1969b) advised: 'Don't listen to the words, just listen to what the voice tells you, what the movements tell you, what the posture tells you . . . The sounds tell you everything . . . the voice is there, the gesture, the posture, the facial expression, the psychosomatic language' (p. 57). Research in gestalt therapy needs to concern itself with this non-verbal behaviour in particular. Interesting possibilities exist in this area. Tomkins (1962, 1963) described the innate patterns of facial expression for each affect, while the universality of facial affect in various western and non-western cultures was supported by Izard (1971) and Ekman (1972, 1977). These investigators would appear to provide a rich background from which researchers of gestalt therapy may choose a topic of interest and relevance.

Episodes are meaningful units of therapeutic interaction designed to achieve an intermediate goal. In gestalt therapy an example of this would be the voicing of criticism by one part of the personality in the three-stage model of conflict resolution outlined by Rice and Greenberg (1982). The relationship level refers to the particular qualities that people attribute to the ongoing interaction that goes beyond any particular act or episode. One of the difficulties in its measurement is the relative paucity of litera-ture on the relational nature of gestalt therapy. The dialogical dimension as outlined by Polster and Polster in Hycner (1987) provides a beginning. The elements which constitute the therapeutic relationship in gestalt therapy need to be identified before appropriate measures can be developed.

A further issue which needs to be addressed arises out of the writing of Perls (1969) concerning the role of self-awareness on the part of clients and the ability to endure unwanted emotions. Awareness on the part of clients was identified by Perls (1969) as essential to change. He stated 'The awareness of, and the ability to endure, unwanted emotions are the conditions, *sine qua non*, for a successful cure' (p. 179). The techniques employed to establish this awareness are the language and non-verbal approaches described in Chapter 4. Studies have yet to be conducted which investigate the effectiveness of these methods in the development of awareness.

The second aspect mentioned by Perls (1969b), namely the ability to endure unwanted emotions, may be more difficult to investigate. Considerable ambiguity surrounds the term emotion. Sometimes it is used interchangeably with the word 'affect' (e.g. Greenberg and Safron, 1987) while at other times the two terms are differentiated (e.g. Rorty, 1980). The role of affect in motivation has been noted by Tomkins (1978). He stated 'The affect system is . . . the primary motivational system because without its amplification, nothing else matters, and with its amplification anything else can matter . . . It lends its power to memory, to perception, to thought, to action' (p. 202).

The role of affect was also highlighted in the work of Demos (1986). She presented a three-stage model of affect involving (a) the triggering event, which can be internal physiological sensations, thoughts, memories or external stimuli; (b) the affective experience *per se*, which involves facial expressions, vocal and respiratory patterns, and autonomic responses; and (c) the response to the affective experience, which can involve the recruitment in memory of past experiences, as well as motor, cognitive and perceptual responses. Although most of Demos' work has been concerned with the infant, the framework which she has adopted would appear to be particularly relevant to the concept of unfinished business in gestalt therapy.

In general, the experiencing of emotions and their expression are considered central to change in gestalt therapy. Little attention has been devoted empirically to this area. Studies need to be conducted which consider (1) the development of emotions, (2) their expression, (3) the particular nature of that expression within gestalt therapy, (4) the process by which clients become aware of emotions, and (5) the relationship between emotions and behaviour.

NEW DIRECTIONS IN RESEARCH METHODS AND ANALYSES

Some of the emerging issues discussed in the previous section require the use of relatively new research methods. For example, episodes require interactional methods for their appropriate investigation. Lag sequential analyses, Markov chain models, information theory, unidirectional and bidirectional tests, tests of dominance, between groups and over-time tests are examples of these.

Lag sequential analysis (Sackett, 1979) assumes that the counselling process is a series of discrete events. It identifies patterns among responses that are temporally distant from one another, thus revealing patterns that are not apparent if the analysis is limited to immediate effects. Both the Markov chain model (cf. Chatfield, 1973) and the information theory approach (cf. Losey, 1978) investigate the structural pattern within the interaction. The order of dependency in the Markov approach and the order of redundancy in the information approach are indices of the pattern. The Markov chain model assumes that the current state of the interaction is contingent upon recent past events, and that the contingency between previous states and the current state is stable over time. The procedure for testing the order of dependency among events under a Markov model is to test a series of models by increasing the events by one in each subsequent model fitting test. It is then possible to predict the dynamics of the interaction. Redundancy in the information theory approach refers to the degree of predictability of events within a sequence. It is assumed that some degree of redundancy occurs in the counsellor–client interaction. It determines patterns based on an increase in information by considering successively larger numbers of antecedent responses.

Unidirectional tests consider the effect of a behaviour by one member of the dyad on either the other or one's own subsequent behaviour. The effect of each person on the other may be investigated simultaneously by means of bidirectional tests (Wampold and Margolin, 1982). A limitation of these tests is that they do not measure dominance, that is, the relative effect of one person's behaviour on the other. Such tests of dominance have been developed by Allison and Liker (1982), Wampold (1984) and Budescu (1984). Wampold (1986) points out that sequential analyses may be used to study different counselling sessions, or one session over time. An index is derived for each interview; these indices are used as dependent measures in traditional inferential tests.

Sequential analyses permit the exploration of both immediate and distal effects. Distal effects can be investigated either within a single session or across multiple sessions. Given the exploratory nature of research in gestalt therapy to date, these methods permit the identification of variables that are important, and those that are unimportant in the therapy process.

In the past, researchers have tended to limit themselves to analyses such as *t*-tests, correlation, ANCOVA and factor analysis. Familiarity with all the analytical tools available is needed to determine which ones are most appropriate in particular circumstances. As gestalt therapy moves to the confirmatory or disconfirmatory phase of analysis, other methods may be employed, such as analysis of covariance (ANCOVA), gain scores, randomized block design, cluster analysis, multiple regression, discriminant analysis, time series and single-subject experiments.

ANCOVA was developed by Fisher (1948) and reduces error variance in randomized experiments (error variance is that part of the observed variance which cannot be accounted for in any other way). ANCOVA is suitable for studies which compare treatment and control groups where pre- and post-treatment measures are available for each subject in both conditions. In ANCOVA, relationships between independent variables and the dependent variable are examined, while the covariables are held constant. This occurs by controlling the relationship of the dependent variables to the covariables. It thus removes the variance in the dependent variables attributable to pretest scores. Porter and Raudenbush (1987) state that ANCOVA is often the most effective way of increasing statistical power, without which the effectiveness of gestalt therapy groups will not be established even when they work.

Two other methods for increasing precision and power include the use of gain scores and the randomized blocks design. Gain scores are post-test–pretest difference scores for each subject. The gain scores are then analysed by ANOVA. However, the error variance for ANCOVA is smaller than that obtained by using gain scores. Furthermore, gain scores can only be used where a pretest has been administered. In ANCOVA any prior information about the subjects may be used as a covariable. Randomized blocks design involves the random assignment of subjects, considered to be similar on the dependent variable, to treatment conditions. It partitions total variation on the dependent variable, removing between-blocks variability from the error variation.

Cluster analysis is a technique which sorts complex data into homogeneous subsets. It allows the partitioning of people or events into relatively distinct groups. Raming and Frey's (1974) study (reported in Chapter 7) illustrates the application of cluster analysis to develop a taxonomy of gestalt processes and goals.

Multiple regression investigates the effects of two or more independent variables (frequently referred to as predictor variables) on a single dependent variable (sometimes designated the criterion variable). The amount of variance in the dependent variable explained or accounted for by the sum of the independent variables is described. Thus we might wish to predict success in therapy on the basis of type of therapy, characteristics of the therapist and type of problem of the client. Multiple regression allows us to do this. Multiple regression is similar to discriminant analysis in that both use a set of predictor variables to estimate a criterion variable. The difference is that whereas multiple regression predicts to a continuous criterion variable, discriminant analysis predicts to a categorical criterion, e.g. group membership.

Use of the time series is recommended where experimental controls are difficult to implement (Campbell and Stanley, 1963). This involves measuring a process at definite intervals and introducing a treatment into this time series of measurements. However, this design suffers from problems of internal validity. It can be hypothesized that some other events produced the shift. The effectiveness of time-series studies is based on the ruling out of such factors. It is desirable that the researcher outlines in advance the expected time relationship between the introduction of the treatment and the manifestation of effect. A single time-series experiment is never conclusive: replications in different settings are needed before conclusions can be drawn.

Randomized single-subject experiments involve the random assignment of treatment times to treatments. However, they do not satisfy the demands of random sampling. Randomization tests are applied in the analysis of data since these tests are valid in the absence of random sampling. They allow reliable inferences to be made on the effect of an experimental treatment on a subject.

Many of the above methods of analysis are dependent on adequate sample size, especially those which are multivariate in nature. The researcher must keep this in mind when determining the statistical methodology to be applied in the analysis of specific data.

CONCLUSION

Research in gestalt therapy is still in its infancy. An exposure to investigative methods and research analysis as part of gestalt therapy training is both desirable and long overdue. This would hopefully result in new research endeavours.

In this chapter, priority areas have been identified which merit the attention of researchers of gestalt therapy. These include replication studies, the development of reliable and valid measures of constructs employed in gestalt therapy, investigations that consider process and outcome simultaneously, and studies that examine various aspects of emotion. The use of randomization, both in the selection of subjects and in their assignment into treatments, has been highlighted. Finally, when analysing and studying findings, it is vital to use appropriate statistical methods in order to ensure that the maximum information gain is achieved.

Chapter 9

Gestalt therapy: a critical evaluation

Gestalt therapy provides a phenomenological framework within which clients can explore polarities or splits in their personalities. It allows them to identify conflicts in their lives, which can then be experienced in a fuller manner than mere reporting would permit. The relating of difficulties can often degenerate into rationalizations or pseudo self-disclosure. Individuals recount facts and circumstances rather than any of the feelings or experiences surrounding the event. They speak of themselves as objects rather than as subjects; gestalt therapy prevents this occurring by focusing primaily on feelings and experiences. Unfinished business from the past can be resolved, freeing individuals to live more fully in their present experience. The basic premise of gestalt therapy is that self-awareness is essential to the integration of the individual. This integration is the conscious acceptance of the wholeness of persons in their disparate elements – thoughts, feelings and physical condition.

Gestalt therapy emphasizes a humanistic, growth-orientated process, as illustrated by the goals outlined in Chapter 2, namely, eliciting personal responsibility and achieving self-integration. In so doing it provides a valuable alternative to psychoanalysis, which stresses the unconscious unknown or symptom. Gestalt therapy uses tangible concrete evidence to achieve positive results. Although acknowledging the intrapsychic factor, from the gestalt therapy viewpoint consideration of the environment is essential. In stressing the quality of client contact, it closely resembles the transactions of transactional analysis. Because of the emphasis on awareness it is akin to existential groups.

As regards degree of structure and division of responsibility, Corey (1985) views gestalt groups as forming the middle of a continuum, which stretches from the non-directiveness of the psychoanalytic and person-centred approaches, to the highly directive structure of many behaviour modification groups. The role of the gestalt leader as an active facilitator has been indicated by the studies of Perls, reported in Chapter 7, yet it is the participants who are responsible for whatever they experience. Kiesler and Goldston's (1988) study (cf. Chapter 7) attests to this freedom, since Gloria was more dominant with Perls than with either Ellis or Rogers.

Gestalt therapy can also be viewed as an integration of behaviouristic and phenomenological approaches. Therapists report their observations of clients' behaviour without interpretation, and may suggest experiments. They allow the clients the freedom to attach meaning to their behaviour. Experiments are enclosed in the experience of clients, and emerge from it. They are carefully graded to the needs of the client, and are viewed as systematic behaviour modifications. By working in the here and now, relevant experiments suggest themselves. Further similarities between behaviourism and gestalt therapy include their emphasis on present behaviour and their lack of concern for explanations. Perls (1969b) stated: 'most people take explaining as being identical with understanding. There is a great difference. I can give you a lot of sentences that help you build an intellectual model of how we function. You wouldn't learn from my words. Learning is discovery' (p. 27).

Unlike other approaches, gestalt therapy lays stress on the affective rather than the cognitive dimension of the human personality. As Perls (1969b) said, 'Lose more and more of your "mind" and come more to your senses'. In this context, however, a distinction must be made between reports of the work in progress and the provision of such explanations after the work has been concluded. Cognition should support the client's experience rather than interfere with it. Hence the meaning of a particular piece of work can be explored once the working through has been completed. 'It is possible to keep your mind and awareness and still "come to your senses"' (Corey, 1986, p. 127).

The suggestion that psychological health involves the ability to move from environmental support to self-support may have profound implications for personal and social relationships. As individuals become more aware of themselves and the quality of their interactions with others, dissatisfaction may occur. What was previously fulfilling may now be unrewarding. For example, introjectors may stop behaving as others wish them to and concentrate on how they themselves want to act. Those to whom they previously gave this control may have difficulty in adjusting to the new situation, and conflict may result. Resolution of this conflict depends largely on the fluidity of the contact boundaries of both parties. However, self-support is not to be confused with self-sufficiency, as Yontef (1987) pointed out. The importance of interdependence and cooperation exists in tandem with self-support.

Gestalt therapy is not for the impatient. It is a slow process of attending to one's experience as it occurs in the present. Perls (1969b) stated that it was not a magic short-cut. Those who are interested in rapid problem solution without considering their own personal growth may find an approach such as reality therapy more satisfying. Shepherd (1970) states: 'Gestalt therapy is most effective with overly socialized, restrained, constricted individuals whose functioning is limited or inconsistent, primarily due to their internal restrictions, and whose enjoyment of living is minimal' (p. 235). Gestalt therapy is particularly useful in dealing with situations from the past which continue to remain in awareness and use up emotional energy. For people who find interaction in group situations difficult, the gestalt group environment provides a safe context in which to explore their difficulties in interaction as well as providing the opportunity to experiment with new behaviours.

Gestalt therapy is being increasingly extended to many situations and problems beyond the merely therapeutic. It is used to enhance the growth of normal college students and professional groups (Fagan and Shepherd, 1970). Dealing with anger and indecision are two particular areas where the use of gestalt therapy appears to be particularly appropriate. However, gestalt therapy may be effective with a variety of both problems and populations. However, as pointed out in Chapter 7, no definite conclusions can be drawn until replication studies have been conducted.

REFERENCES

Allison, P.D. and Liker, J.K. (1982) Analyzing sequential categorical data on dyadic interaction, comment on Guttman. *Psychological Bulletin*, **91**, 393–403.

Anderson, J.D. (1978) Growth groups and alienation: a comparative study of Rogerian encounter, self-directed encounter and gestalt. *Group and Organisation Studies*, **3**, 85–107.

Bandler, R. and Grinder, J. (1975, 1979) *The Structure of Magic*, Science and Behavior Books, Palo Alto, CA.

Barrett-Lennard, G.T. (1962) Dimensions of therapists' response as causal factors in therapeutic change. *Psychological Monograph*, **76**, 562.

Battle, C.C., Imber, S.D. and Hochsnar, R. (1966) Target complaints as criteria of improvement. *American Journal of Psychotherapy*, **20**, 184–92.

Benjamin, L.S. (1979) Use of structural analysis of social behaviour (SASB) and Markov chains to study dyadic interaction. *Journal of Abnormal Psychology*, **88**, 303–19.

Berne, E. (1967) *Games People Play*. Grove Press, New York.

Berzon, B. and Reisel, J. (1976) *Effective Interpersonal Relationships*. La Jolla, CA.

Bloxom, B. (1985) The personal orientation inventory. In Mitchell, J.V. (ed) *The Ninth Mental Measurement Yearbook*. University of Nebraska Press, Nebraska, pp. 290–2.

Boring, E. (1950) *A History of Experimental Psychology*. Appleton-Century-Crofts, New York.

Bouchard, M., Lecomte, C., Carbonneau, H. and Lalonde, F. (1987) Inferential communication of expert psychoanalytically oriented, gestalt and behaviour therapists. *Canadian Journal of Behavior Science*, **19**, 275–86.

Buber, M. (1965) *Between Man and Man* (Trans. R.G. Smith). Macmillan Books, New York.

Byrne, D. (1964) Repression – sensitization as a dimension of personality, in *Progress in Experimental Personality Research (vol 1)*, (Ed. B.A. Mahrer), Academic Press, New York.

Campbell, D.T. and Stanley, J.C. (1963) Experimental and quasi-experimental designs for research on teaching. In Gage, L. (ed) *Handbook of Research and Teaching*. Rand McNally, Chicago, pp. 171–246.

Chatfield, C. (1973) Statistical inference regarding Markov chain models, *Applied Statistics*, **22**, 7–20.

Clarke, K.M. and Greenberg, L.S. (1986) Differential effects of the gestalt two-chair intervention and problem solving in resolving decisional conflict. *Journal of Counselling Psychology*, **53**, 11–15.

Clarkson, P. (1989) *Gestalt Counselling in Action*. Sage, London.

Coan, R.W. (1985) The Personal Orientation Inventory. In Mitchell, J.V. (ed) *The Ninth Mental Measurement Yearbook*. University of Nebraska Press, Nebraska, pp. 292–4.

Cohn, R.C. (1970) Therapy in groups: psychoanalytic, experimental and gestalt. In Fagan, J. and Shepherd, I. (eds) *Gestalt Therapy Now*. Science and Behavior Books, Palo Alto, CA, pp. 130–39.

Conoley, C.W., Conoley, J.C., McConnell, J.A. and Kimzey, C.G. (1983) The effects of the ABCs of rational emotive therapy and the empty-chair technique of gestalt therapy on anger reduction. *Psychotherapy: Theory, Research and Practice*, **20**, 112–17.

Corey, G. (1985, 1986) *Theory and Practice of Group Counselling*. Brooks/Cole, Monterey, CA.

Côté, N. (1982) Effects of an intensive gestalt session on the level of self-actualization and the personality structure, *Gestalt Theory*, **4**, 89–106.

Davis, R.V. (1987) Scale construction. *Journal of Counselling Psychology*, **34**, 418–89.

Demos, V. (1986) Crying in early infancy. In Brazelton, T.B. and Yogman M.W. (eds) *Affective Development in Infancy*. Ablex, New Jersey, pp. 39–73.

Dempsey, P. (1961) *Psychology for All*. Mercier Press, Cork.

Dryden, W. (1984) *Individual Therapy in Britain*. Harper and Row, London.

Ekman, P. (1972) Universal and cultural differences in facial expression of emotion. *Nebraska Symposium on Motivation*, **19**, 207–83.

Ekman, P. (1977) Biological and cultural contributions to body and facial movement. In Blacking, J. (ed) *Anthropology of the Body*. Academic Press, London, pp. 39–84.

Enright, J. (1970) An introduction to gestalt techniques. In Fagan, J. and Shephard, I. (eds) *Gestalt Therapy Now: Theory, Techniques and Application*. Science and Behavior Books, Palo Alto, CA, pp. 107–24.

Fagan, J. and Shepherd, I. (1970) *Gestalt Therapy Now*. Science and Behavior Books, Palo Alto.

Fagan, J., Lauver, D., Smith, S. *et al.* (1974) Critical incidents in the empty chair. *The Counselling Psychologist*, **4**, 33–42.

Fensterheim, H. and Baer, J. (1976) *Don't say yes when you want to say no*, Futura, London.

Fisher, R.A. (1948) *Statistical Methods for Research Workers*, 10th ed. Hafner, New York.

Foulds, M.L. and Hannigan, P.S. (1976a) Gestalt marathon workshop: effects on extraversion and neuroticism, *Journal of College Student Personnel*, **17**, 50–4.

Foulds, M.L. and Hannigan, P.S. (1976b) Effects of gestalt marathon workshops on measured self-actualization: a replication and follow-up study. *Journal of Counselling Psychology*, **23**, 60–5.

Foulds, M.L. and Hannigan, P.S. (1977) Gestalt workshop and measured changes in self-actualization; replication and refinement study. *Journal of College Student Personnel*, **18**, 200–5.

Freud, S. (1900) *The Interpretation of Dreams*, standard editions 4 and 5 of The Complete Psychological Works of Sigmund Freud, Hogarth Press, London.

Freud, S. (1975) *The Interpretation of Dreams*. (Tr. A. Richards). Basic Books, New York.

Frew, J.E. (1986) The functions and patterns of occurrences of individual contact styles during the developmental phases of the gestalt group. *Gestalt Journal*, **9**, 55–70.

Friedman, M. (1990) Dialogue philosophical anthropology and gestalt therapy. *Gestalt Journal*, **13**, 7–40.

Friedman, M. and Rosenman, R. (1974) *Type A Behaviour and Your Heart*. Wildwood Press, London.

Gaines, J. (1979) *Fritz Perls Here and Now*. Celestial Arts, Millbrae, CA.

Gendlin, E. (1968) Focusing ability in psychotherapy, personality and creativity. In Shlien, J. (ed) *Research in Psychotherapy*, Vol. III. American Psychological Association, Washington.

Gendlin, E. (1978) *Focusing*. (USA) Bantam Books, Toronto.

Glasser, W. (1984) *Control Theory*. Harper and Row, New York.

Gough, H.G. and Heilbrun, A.B. (1965) *The Adjective Check-List Manual*. Consulting Psychologists Press, Palo Alto, CA.

Goulding, R. and Goulding M. (1979) *Changing Lives Through Redecision Therapy*. Brunner/Mazel, New York.

Greenberg, L.S. (1983) Toward a task analysis of conflict resolution in gestalt therapy. *Psychotherapy: Theory, Research and Practice*, **8**, 310–14.

Greenberg, L.S. (1986) Change process research, *Journal of Consulting and Clinical Psychology*, **54**, 4–9.

Greenberg, L.S. and Clarke, K.M. (1979) Differential effects of the two-chair experiment and empathic reflection at a conflict marker. *Journal of Counselling Psychology*, **26**, 1–8.

Greenberg, L.S. and Dompierre, L.M. (1981) Specific effects of gestalt two-chair dialogue in intrapsychic conflict in counselling, *Psychology*, **28**, 288–94.

Greenberg, L.S. and Higgins, H.M. (1980) Effects of two-chair dialogue and focusing on conflict resolution. *Journal of Counselling Psychology*, **27**, 221–4.

Greenberg, L.S. and Rice, L.N. (1981) The specific effects of a gestalt intervention. *Psychotherapy: Theory, Research and Practice*, **18**, 31–7.

Greenberg, L.S. and Webster, M.C. (1982) Resolving decisional conflict by gestalt two-chair dialogue: relating process to outcome. *Journal of Counselling Psychology*, **20**, 468–77.

Guinan, J.F. and Foulds, M.L. (1970) Marathon group: facilitator of personal growth. *Journal of Counselling Psychology*, **17**, 145–9.

Gurman, A.S. and Razim, A.M. (1977) *Effective Psychotherapy: A Research Handbook*. Pergamon Press, Oxford.

Harman, R. (1982) Working at the contact boundaries. *Gestalt Journal S.*, **5**, 39–48.

Harren, V.A. (1979) A model of career decision making for college students. *Journal of Vocational Behaviour*, **14**, 119–33.

Hatcher, C. and Himelstein, P. (1976) *Handbook of Gestalt Therapy*. Jason Aronson, New York.

Hill, C.E., Thames, T.B. and Rardin, D.K. (1979) Comparison of Rogers, Perls and Hills on the Hill Counsellor Verbal Response Category System. *Journal of Counselling Psychology*, **26**, 198–203.

Hinksman, B. (1988) Gestalt group therapy. In Aveline, M. and Dryden, W. (eds) *Group Therapy in Britain*. Open University Press, Milton Keynes, pp. 65–82.

Houston, G. (1990) *Supervision in Counselling*. Rochester Foundation, London.

Howard, G.S. (1982) Improving methodology via research on research methods. *Journal of Counselling Psychology*, **29**, (3), 318–26.

Hycner, R.A. (1990) The I–Thou relationship and gestalt therapy. *Gestalt Journal*, **13**, 41–54.

Izard, C.E. (1971) *The Face of Emotions*, Appleton-Century-Crofts, New York.

James, W. (1890) *Principles of Psychology*. Holt, Rinehart and Winston, New York.

James, M. and Jongeward, D. (1971) *Born to Win*. Signet, New York.

Kepner, J.I. (1987) *Body Process*. Gestalt Institute of Cleveland Press, New York.

Kepner, E. and Brien, L. (1970) Gestalt therapy: a behavioristic phenomenology. In Fagan, J. and Shepherd, I.L. (eds) *Gestalt Therapy Now*. Harper and Row, New York.

Kierkegaard, S. (1944) *The Concept of Dread*. Princeton University Press, Princeton, N.J.

Kiresuk, T. and Sherman, R. (1968) Goal attainment scaling: a general method for evaluating comprehensive community mental health programmes. *Community Mental Health Journal*, **4**, 443–53.

Klien, M., Mathieu, P., Gendlin, E. and Kiesler, E. (1969) *The Experiencing Scale*. Wisconsin Psychiatric Institute, Madison, Wis.

Krauss, H.N., Ruiz, R.A., Mozdzierz, G.J. and Button, J. (1967) Anxiety and temporal perspective among normals in a stressful life situation. *Psychological Reports*, **21**, 721–4.

Kubler-Ross, E. (1984) *On Death and Dying*. Routledge, London.

LaForge, R. and Suczek, R.F. (1955) The interpersonal dimension of personality III. An interpersonal checklist. *Journal of Personality*, **24**, 92–112.

Laing, R.D., Phillipson, H. and Lee, A.R. (1966) *Interpersonal Perception: a Theory and Method of Research*. Springer, New York.

Latner, J. (1982) The thresher of time: on love and freedom in gestalt therapy. *Gestalt Journal*, **5**, 20–38.

Lieberman, M.A., Yalom, I.D. and Miles, M.B. (1973) *Encounter Groups: First Facts*. Basic Books, New York.

Losey, G. (1978) Information theory and communication. In Colgan, P. (ed) *Quantitative Ethology*. Wiley, New York, pp. 43–78.

Lynd, M.M. (1958) *On Shame and the Search for Identity*. Science Editions, New York.

McQuilty, L.L. (1970) Hierarchical classification by multiple linkages. *Educational and Psychological Measurement*, **30**, 3–19.

Maslow, A.M. (1956) *Towards a Psychology of Being*. Van Nostrand, New York.

Meara, N.M., Shannon, J.W. and Pepinsky, H.B. (1979) Comparison of the stylistic complexity of the language of counsellor and client across three theoretical orientations. *Journal of Counselling Psychology*, **26**, 181–9.

Meier, J.T. and Davis, S.R. (1990) Trends in reporting psychometric properties of scales used in counselling psychological research. *Journal of Counselling Psychology*, **37**, 113–15.

Mercier, M.A. and Johnson, M. (1984) Representational system predicate use and convergence in counselling: Gloria revisited. *Journal of Counselling Psychology*, **31**, 161–9.

Mermin, D. (1974) Gestalt theory of emotion. *Counselling Psychologist*, 15–21.

llham, J. and Jacobsen, L.I. (1978) The need for approval. In London, H. and Exner, J. (eds) *Dimensions of Personality*. Wiley, New York.

tchell, J.V. (1985) *The Ninth Mental Measurement Yearbook*, University of Nebraska Press, Nebraska.

oreno, J.L. (1946) *Psychodrama*. Beacon House, New York.

oustakas, C. (1974) *The Self: Explorations in Personal Growth*. Harper and Row, New York.

urgatroyd, S. (1985) *Counselling and Helping*, British Psychological Society and Methuen, London.

aranjo, C. (1970) Present-centredness: technique, prescription and ideal. In Fagan, J. and Shepherd, I.L. (eds) *Gestalt Therapy Now*. Science and Behavior Books, Palo Alto, pp. 47–69.

aranjo, C. (1980) The techniques of gestalt therapy. *Gestalt Journal*, Highland, New York.

elson, W.M. and Groman W.D. (1975) Neurotic verbalizations: an exploration of gestalt therapy assumptions. *Journal of Clinical Psychology*, **31**, 732–7.

elson, W.M. and Groman, W.D. (1978) Temporal perspective from the gestalt therapy assumption of present-centredness. *Psychotherapy: Theory, Research and Practice*, **15**, 277–84.

Leary, E. (1986) *The Psychology of Counselling*, 2nd edn. Cork University Press, Cork.

Leary, E. and Martin, A. (1989) Gestalt therapy. *Institute of Guidance Counsellors Journal*, **15**, 13–17.

Leary, E. and Page, R. (1990) An evaluation of a person-centred gestalt group using the semantic differential. *Counselling Psychology Quarterly*, **3**, 13–21.

ipow, S.H., Carney, C.G. and Barak, W. (1976) A scale of educational–vocational undecidedness: A typological approach. *Journal of Behaviour*, **9**, 233–43.

ge, F. (1984) Gestalt therapy. In Dryden, W. (ed) *Individual Therapy in Britain*, Harper and Row, London, pp. 180–204.

ssons, W. (1975) *Gestalt Approaches in Counselling*. Holt, Rinehart and Winston, New York.

tterson, C.H. (1973) *Theories of Counselling and Psychotherapy*. Harper and Row, New York.

rls, F. (1967) Group vs. individual therapy, *Review of General Semantics*, **34**, 306–12.

rls, F.S. (1969a) *In and Out of the Garbage Pail*. Real People Press, Lafayette, CA.

rls, F.S. (1969b) *Gestalt Therapy Verbatim*. Bantam, Toronto.

rls, F.S. (1970) Dream seminars. In Fagan, J. and Shepherd, I. (eds) *Gestalt Therapy Now*. Science and Behavior Books, Palo Alto, pp. 204–33.

rls, F.S. (1973) *The Gestalt Approach and Eye Witness to Therapy*. Science and Behavior Books, Palo Alto.

rls, F.S. (1975) Morality, ego boundary and aggression. In Stevens, J.O. and Stevens, B. (eds) *Gestalt Is*. Real People Press, Utah, pp. 27–37.

rls, L. (1976) Comments on new directions. In Smith, E.L. (ed) *The Growing Edge of Gestalt Therapy*. Brunner/Mazel, New York, pp. 221–6.

rls, F., Hefferline, R. and Goodman, P. (1951) *Gestalt Therapy*. Julian Press, New York.

tterson, G. and Bradley, R.W. (1980) Counsellor orientation and theoretical attitudes toward counselling: historical perspective and data. *Journal of Counselling Psychology*, **27**, 554–60.

olster, E. (1987) *Every Person's Life is Worth a Novel*. Norton and Co, New York.

Polster, E. and Polster, M. (1973) *Gestalt Therapy Integrated*. Vintage Books, New York.

Porter, A.C. and Raudenbush, S.W. (1987) Analysis of co-variance, its model and use in psychological research. *Journal of Counselling Psychology*, **34**, 383–92.

Powell, J. (1976) *Fully Human, Fully Alive*. Argus, Niles, Illinois.

Rainwater, J. (1976) *You're in Charge! A Guide to Becoming Your Own Therapist*. Guild of Tutors Press, Los Angeles.

Raming, H.E. and Frey, D.H. (1974) A taxonomic approach to the gestalt theory of Perls. *Journal of Counselling Psychology*, **21**, 179–84.

Reich, W. (1969) *Character Analysis*. (Tr. T. Wolfe). Vision Press, London.

Rice, L. and Greenberg, L. (1982) *Patterns of Change: Intensive Analysis of Psychotherapy Process*. Guilford, New York.

Rice, L., Koke, C., Greenberg, L. and Wagstaff, A. (1979) *Voice Quality Training Manual*. Counselling and Development Centre Press, Toronto.

Rice, L. and Wagstaff, A. (1967) Client voice quality and expressive style: two indices of productive psychotherapy. *Journal of Consulting Psychology*, **31**, 557–63.

Rogers, C.R. (1961) *On Becoming a Person*. Constable, London.

Rorty, A.D. (1980) *Explaining Emotions*. University of California Press, Berkeley.

Rosenberg, M. (1965) *Society and the Adolescent Self-image*. Princeton University Press, Princeton, NJ.

Rosenblatt, D. (1975) *Gestalt Therapy Primer*. Harper and Row, New York.

Rosenblatt, D. (1976) *Your Life is a Mess*. Harper and Row, New York.

Rosenblatt, D. (1980) The dynamic process of support contact. *Gestalt Journal*, **3**, 64–8.

Rosenfeld, E. (1978) An oral history of gestalt therapy: part one. *Gestalt Journal*, **1**, 9–28.

Sackett, G. (1979) The lag sequential analysis of contingency and cyclicity in behavioural interaction research. In Osofsky, J. (ed) *Handbook of Infant Development*, Wiley, New York, pp. 623–49.

Sahakian, W.S. (1976) *Psychotherapy and Counselling*. Rand McNally, Chicago.

Satir, V. (1976) *Making Contact*. Celestial Arts, Berkeley.

Shepard, M. (1976) *Fritz*. Bantam Books, New York.

Shepherd, J.L. (1970) Limitations and cautions in the gestalt approach. In Fagan, J. and Shepherd, J.L. (eds) *Gestalt Therapy Now*. Harper and Row, New York, pp. 234–8.

Shlien, J.M. (1984) Secrets and the psychology of secrecy. In Levant, R.F. and Shlien, J.M. (eds) *Client-centred Therapy and the Person-centred Approach*. Praeger, New York.

Shostrom, E.L. (1966) *Personal Orientation Inventory*. Educational and Industrial Testing Service, San Diego.

Smith, E. (1986) Retroflection: the forms of non-enactment. *Gestalt Journal*, **9**, 36–54.

Smith, E.W.L. (1977) *The Growing Edge of Gestalt Therapy*, The Citadel Press, Secaucus, NJ.

Smith, M.L., Glass, G.V. and Miller, T.I. (1980) *The Benefits of Psychotherapy*. John Hopkins University, Baltimore.

Sobel, B.J. (1979) Preferences for behavioural, analytic and gestalt psychotherapy. *British Journal of Medical Psychology*, **52**, 263–9.

Stevens, J.O. (1971) *Awareness: Exploring, Experimenting, Experiencing*. Real People Press, Utah.

Swain, R. (1989) Effects of a 7-hour gestalt group on student self-esteem and class cohesiveness. *Journal of Higher Education Studies*, **4**, 23–6.

)bin, S. (1975) Saying goodbye, in *Gestalt Is*, (Ed. J.O. Stevens), Real People Press, Utah.

>mkins, S. (1962) *Affect, Imagery, Consciousnes, Vol. 1. The Positive Affects*. Springer, New York.

>mkins, S. (1963) *Affect, Imagery, Consciousness, Vol. 2. The Negative Affects*. Springer, New York.

>mkins, S. (1978) Script theory: differential magnification of affects. *Nebraska Symposium on Motivation*, **26**, 201–36.

'son, G.M. and Range, L.M. (1987) Gestalt dialogues as a treatment for mild depression: time works just as well. *Journal of Clinical Psychology*, **43**, 227–31.

in de Riet, V., Korb, M.E. and Gorrell, J.J. (1988) Gestalt Therapy: an Introduction. Pergamon Press, New York.

ampold, B.E. (1984) Tests of dominance in sequential categorical data. *Psychological Bulletin*, **96**, 424–9.

ampold, B.E. (1986) State of the art in sequential analysis. *Journal of Counselling Psychology*, **33**(2), 182–4.

>odworth, R. and Schlosberg, H. (1954) *Experimental Psychology*. Holt, Rinehart and Winston, New York.

n, R.K. and Heald, K.A. (1975) Using the case survey method to analyse policy studies. *Administrative Science Quarterly*, **20**, 371–81.

n, R.K., Bingham, E. and Heald, K.A. (1976) The difference that quality makes. *Sociological Methods and Research*, **5**, 139–56.

)ntef, G. (1987) Gestalt therapy: a polemic. *Gestalt Journal*, **10**, 41–68.

mmer, J.M. and Cowles, K.M. (1972) Content analysis using Fortran: applied to interviews conducted by C. Rogers, F. Perls and A. Ellis. *Journal of Counselling Psychology*, **19**, 161–6.

nker, J. (1978) *Creative Process in Gestalt Therapy*. Vintage, New York.

nker, J. (1979) Telling tales about the old master, *Gestalt Journal*, **2**, 24–34.

nker, J. (1981) Comment. In Perls, L., Polster, M., Yontef, G. and Zinker, J. (eds) The future of gestalt therapy; a symposium. *Gestalt Journal*, **4**, 3–18.

FURTHER READING

merican Association of Counselling and Development (1989) Responsibilities of users of standardized tests (RUST), AACD, Alex:Va.

own, J. (1986) *I only want what's best for you*, Cedar, London.

unink, S.A. and Schroeder, H.W. (1970) Verbal therapeutic behaviours of expert psychoanalytically oriented, gestalt and behaviour therapists, *Journal of Consulting and Clinical Psychology*, **47**, 567–74.

idescu, D.V. (1984) Tests of lagged dominance in sequential dyadic interaction, *Psychological Bulletin*, **96**, 402–14.

)oley, C.M. (1902) *Human Nature and the Social Order*, Scribners Press, New York.

reenberg, L.S. and Safran, J.D. (1987) *Emotion and Psychotherapy*, Guilford Press, New York.

eidbreder, S. (1961) *Seven Psychologies*, Appleton-Century-Crofts, New York.

eidegger, M. (1968) *Existence and Being*, Vision Press, London.

ill, D.C. (1987) The relationship of process to outcome in brief expressive psychotherapy, *Dissertation Extracts International*, **47**(9), 3259-A.

)uston, G. (1980) *The Red Book of Gestalt*, Rochester Foundation, London.

Hycner, R. (1987) An interview with Erving and Miriam Polster, *Gestalt Journal*, **13**, 41–54.

Izard, C.E. (1968) The emotions and emotional constructs in personality and cultural research, in *Handbook of Modern Personality Theory* (ed. R.B. Cattel), Aldine, Chicago.

Jesse, R.E. and Guerney, B.G. (1981) A comparison of gestalt and relationship enhancement treatments with married couples, *American Journal of Family Therapy*, **9**(3), 31–41.

Kempler, W. (1974) Gestalt therapy, in *Current Psychotherapies*, 2nd edn (ed. R.J. Corsini), Itasca Press.

Kiesler, D.J. and Goldston, C.S. (1988) Client–therapist complementality: an analysis of the Gloria films, *Journal of Counselling Psychology*, **35**, 427–33.

Lamper, N. (1971a) The village idiot, *Voices*, **8**, 66–7.

Lamper, N. (1971b) The healing hands of Cowichan, *Psychotherapy: Theory, Research and Practice*, **8**, 310–14.

Levitsky, A. and Perls, F.S. (1970) The rules and games of gestalt therapy, in *Gestalt Therapy Now* (eds. J. Fagan and I.L. Shepherd), Science and Behaviour Books, Palo Alto, CA, pp. 140–9.

Miller, C.M. (1980) An experimental study of the effects of the gestalt two-chair experiment with conflicted adolescent offenders, *Dissertation Abstracts International*, **41**(10), 4291A.

Perls, F.S. (1947) *Ego Hunger and Aggression*, Vintage Books, New York.

Polster, E. and Polster, M. (1979) An oral history of gestalt therapy, Part 3: a conversation with Erving and Miriam Polster (conducted by Jo Wysong), *Gestalt Journal*, **2**, 3–26.

Rosenberg, M. (1989) Citation classic: determinants of self-esteem, *Current Contents – Social and Behavioural Sciences*, **21**(II), 16.

Rosenblatt, D. (1975) *Opening Doors*, Perennial Library, New York.

Shostrom, E.L. (1964) *Three Approaches to Psychotherapy*, Psychological Films, Santa Ana, CA.

Wampold, B.E. and Margolin, G. (1982) Nonparametric strategies to test the independence of behavioural states in sequential data, *Psychological Bulletin*, **92**, 755–65.

Index